Decoding the Markets:
A Practical Guide to Technical Indicators

John Connor

Table of Contents

Dedication

To my beloved wife and partner, Patti Connor, thank you for sharing this incredible journey with me. From our fateful blind date when you were just 19 to navigating the twists and turns of mid-life together, your unwavering support has been my anchor. As I worked on this book, your encouragement served as a guiding light. You offered invaluable ideas and insights, diligently reading through every draft and helping me make sense of the chaos. Patti, you are more than just a wonderful partner; you are my confidante, my inspiration, and my greatest love. Thank you for these wonderful years. LUV!!!

Preface

In an industry marked by volatility and constant change, John Michael Connor stands out for his adaptability and experience. His career reflects a steady commitment to thriving in the ever-evolving world of finance, navigating its complexities with strategic focus and dedication to excellence.

Connor began his journey on the bustling trading floor of the Chicago Mercantile Exchange, where he quickly developed skills in the high-pressure world of open outcry trading. As the financial landscape shifted toward computerized clearing, he transitioned smoothly, staying ahead of industry changes. His knowledge of algorithmic trading and risk management has continued to guide his success and set a strong example in the field.

Throughout his career, Connor has crafted and implemented effective trading strategies across a range of asset classes, regularly meeting and exceeding client expectations. His ability to manage market complexities and risk while enhancing portfolio performance has earned him the trust of both clients and colleagues.

What truly distinguishes Connor is his interpersonal approach. He excels at building lasting client relationships, customizing investment strategies, and providing clear financial reports. His skill in explaining complex financial concepts in an approachable way has made him a reliable advisor and valued partner.

Connor's drive for growth is reflected in his education and career path. With a Liberal Arts degree and a minor in Business from Indiana State University, he built a strong base in problem-solving and decision-making. As publisher of the Market Watch Bulletin, he offered insights into the Chicago futures market, deepening his understanding of finance.

Connor's professional journey includes contributions to firms like Alpha Z Advisors, Cunningham Commodities, LLC, and Futures & Options Execution LLC. His leadership roles at Chicago Capital Management LLC, where he directed trading strategies and ensured regulatory compliance, highlight his ability to oversee complex operations effectively.

This book captures John Michael Connor's dedication, practical insights, and expertise in finance. His experiences offer a valuable guide for anyone looking to navigate the financial landscape, adapt to change, and achieve success in their own endeavors.

Chapter 1:

Introduction to Technical Analysis

In the ever-evolving world of financial markets, the ability to accurately analyze and predict price movements is a skill that separates successful traders from the rest. For anyone serious about trading—whether in stocks, Forex, commodities, or even cryptocurrencies—technical analysis is a crucial tool. At its core, technical analysis involves using historical price and volume data to forecast future price movements, relying on charts, patterns, and various technical indicators. Understanding this analytical approach is key to developing a comprehensive trading strategy that enhances decision-making and profitability. "The best thing about the future is that it only comes one day at a time." - Abraham Lincoln

This chapter will introduce you to the fundamentals of technical analysis, the significance of trading indicators, and their role in decoding price movements. We will explore the principles that underpin technical analysis, the most commonly used charts and patterns, and why mastering this analytical approach is essential for any aspiring trader.

The Fundamentals of Technical Analysis

Technical analysis is founded on the principle that price movements in financial markets follow identifiable patterns and trends, and that history tends to repeat itself. Rather than focusing on the intrinsic value of an asset, as in fundamental analysis, technical analysis is purely concerned with the behavior of prices in the marketplace. This methodology assumes that all relevant factors that could influence an asset's price—be it economic news, political events, or market sentiment—are already reflected in its current price.

Charles Dow, often regarded as the father of technical analysis, laid the groundwork for this field in the late 19th century through his *Dow Theory*. According to Dow, market prices move in trends, and by studying these trends, traders can make educated predictions about future price behavior. Dow's work emphasized the cyclical nature of market movements, observing that prices rise and fall in discernible patterns, which technical analysts aim to identify and exploit.

Unlike fundamental analysis, which examines a company's financial health, earnings, and industry position, technical analysis assumes that everything traders need to know is already visible in the price action. By studying price charts and volume data, traders seek to detect these trends and patterns early, positioning themselves to either follow the market momentum or capitalize on potential reversals.

The Core Principles of Technical Analysis

Several key principles form the foundation of technical analysis. Understanding these principles will allow you to grasp why traders rely so heavily on this method to interpret market behavior and make trading decisions:

- **Price Reflects All Information**: This is the central tenet of technical analysis. It asserts that the price of a financial asset reflects every factor that could influence it—be it political events, economic reports, earnings results, or even speculative sentiment. Therefore, by analyzing price movements, traders are effectively interpreting all available information.

- **Price Movements Are Not Random**: According to technical analysis, prices tend to move in trends—upward (bullish), downward (bearish), or sideways (ranging). A trader's primary task is to identify these trends as early as possible and trade accordingly. Technical analysts believe that markets are driven by human psychology and herd behavior, causing trends to persist until external factors disrupt them.

- **History Repeats Itself**: Another foundational principle is the belief that historical price behavior tends to repeat. Traders recognize recurring patterns in price charts—such as head and shoulders, flags, or double bottoms—that signal future price movements. These patterns are considered reliable because they have been observed repeatedly over decades of market behavior.

By adhering to these principles, technical analysts develop a methodical approach to forecasting price changes, helping them identify trading opportunities and manage risks. "Risk is what keeps us young." - Wall Street: Money Never Sleeps (2010)

The Role of Indicators in Analyzing Price Movements

Indicators play an indispensable role in technical analysis. These are mathematical calculations derived from price, volume, or open interest, and they offer traders additional insights into market behavior that go beyond what can be seen on price charts alone. Indicators can help traders determine whether a market is trending, whether it is overbought or oversold, and whether a potential reversal is imminent.

There are two main types of indicators: leading indicators and lagging indicators.

- **Leading Indicators**: These indicators attempt to predict future price movements, providing signals before a trend or reversal begins. Leading indicators are particularly useful for traders who want to catch the start of a new trend or capitalize on a market reversal. Popular leading indicators include the Relative Strength Index (RSI) and the Stochastic Oscillator, both of which help traders determine whether an asset is overbought or oversold, potentially signaling a reversal.

- **Lagging Indicators**: In contrast to leading indicators, lagging indicators provide signals after a trend has started and are typically used to confirm the strength of the trend. These indicators are useful for traders who want to ensure that a trend is well-established before entering a trade. Moving Averages, such as the Simple Moving Average (SMA) and the Exponential Moving Average (EMA), are common lagging indicators used to smooth out price data and identify the overall direction of the trend.

Types of Price Charts and How They Inform Trading Decisions

One of the most important tools in technical analysis is the price chart. These charts visually represent the historical price movements of a financial asset, allowing traders to detect trends, patterns, and potential entry or exit points. There are several types of price charts that traders use, each offering unique insights:

- **Line Charts**: These are the simplest type of price charts, displaying a line that connects the closing prices of an asset over a given time period. Line charts provide a clear view of the overall direction of an asset's price, making them ideal for long-term traders who are less concerned with the minutiae of daily price fluctuations.

- **Bar Charts**: Bar charts provide more information than line charts, as they display the opening, closing, high, and low prices for each trading session. Each bar on the chart represents a specific time period (e.g., one day or one hour), with the top of the bar representing the highest price and the bottom representing the lowest. A small horizontal line on the left side of the bar shows the opening price, while the one on the right shows the closing price. Bar charts are particularly useful for short-term traders who need to see detailed price action over time.

- **Candlestick Charts**: Perhaps the most popular type of price chart among traders, candlestick charts provide the same data as bar charts but in a more visually intuitive format. Each candlestick on the chart represents a specific time period and shows the opening, closing, high, and low prices. The body of the candlestick is color-coded to show whether the price moved up or down during the time period, with green (or white) representing upward movement and red (or black) representing downward movement. The "wicks" (or shadows) of the candlestick represent the high and low prices during the session.

Candlestick charts are highly effective for spotting patterns, such as **doji**, **hammer**, and **engulfing patterns**, all of which signal potential reversals or continuations in the market.

Time Frames and Their Impact on Trading Strategies

Technical analysis can be applied across various time frames, from the one-minute chart used by day traders to the monthly or yearly charts favored by long-term investors. The time frame you choose will largely depend on your trading style and objectives:

- **Day Traders**: Typically, day traders rely on very short time frames, such as one-minute or five-minute charts. Their goal is to capitalize on small price movements throughout the trading day, often entering and exiting positions within a matter of minutes or hours. In this case, technical indicators that provide quick, actionable signals—like the RSI or moving averages—are essential for identifying opportunities in real time.

- **Swing Traders**: Swing traders hold positions for several days to weeks, seeking to profit from medium-term price trends. They usually rely on daily or four-hour charts and use technical indicators like MACD (Moving Average Convergence Divergence) or Bollinger Bands to detect market momentum and volatility. Cut your losses short. Let your profits run.

- **Position Traders**: Position traders are long-term investors who may hold assets for months or even years. They typically rely on weekly or monthly charts to spot long-term trends. Position traders often combine technical analysis with fundamental analysis to identify undervalued assets and ride major market movements.

Support and Resistance Levels: The Building Blocks of Trading Decisions

Two of the most important concepts in technical analysis are support and resistance levels. Support is a price level where demand for an asset is strong enough to prevent the price from falling further. When an asset's price approaches a support level, it tends to bounce upward as buyer's step in. Conversely, resistance is a price level where selling pressure increases, preventing the price from rising further. When an asset's price reaches a resistance level, it typically pulls back as sellers take profits. "Buy low, sell high. Fear? That's the other guy's problem." - Trading Places (1983)

Support and resistance levels act as psychological barriers in the market, influencing traders' behavior. Traders use these levels to set entry and exit points, often placing stop-loss orders just below support or just above resistance. Breaking through these levels can lead to significant price movements, as the breach of support or resistance is often seen as a signal that the market is entering a new phase.

For example, in 2020, when the price of Bitcoin broke through its previous all-time high of $20,000, it triggered a massive buying frenzy, leading to a new rally that took the cryptocurrency to over $60,000 within a few months. Identifying such breakout points is a key application of technical analysis.

The Advantages and Limitations of Technical Analysis

There are several reasons why technical analysis remains popular among traders. First and foremost, it offers clarity in interpreting price action. With the use of charts, indicators, and patterns, traders can cut through the noise of the market and focus on objective data rather than being swayed by emotions or external influences. This data-driven approach allows for more disciplined trading. Richard Dennis - "Trading decisions should be made as unemotionally as possible."

Second, technical analysis can be applied to virtually any market, making it a versatile tool. Whether you're trading stocks, currencies, commodities, or even cryptocurrencies, the principles of technical analysis remain the same. This universal applicability is one of the reasons why traders across the globe rely on it.

However, technical analysis is not without its limitations. One of the primary criticisms is its subjectivity. Different traders may interpret the same price chart or indicator in different ways, leading to conflicting opinions on the market's direction. This subjectivity can make it challenging for new traders to develop confidence in their analysis.

Additionally, technical analysis is based on historical data, and while price patterns often repeat, there are no guarantees that they will in the future. As the adage goes, "past performance is not indicative of future results." Markets can change rapidly due to unforeseen events, such as political upheavals, natural disasters, or sudden economic shocks, rendering previous patterns irrelevant.

Another limitation is the potential for false signals. Leading indicators, while useful for anticipating market movements, can sometimes provide misleading information. For instance, the RSI may indicate that an asset is overbought, suggesting a reversal, but the price may continue to rise for some time before correcting. Traders need to use indicators cautiously and in conjunction with other tools to minimize the risk of false signals.

Finally, technical analysis does not account for fundamental factors that may influence an asset's price. While technical analysis is powerful, ignoring economic reports, earnings releases, or geopolitical events can leave traders blind to important market shifts. Many successful traders combine both technical and fundamental analysis to create a more holistic trading strategy.

In summary, technical analysis is an invaluable tool for traders, providing a structured approach to interpreting price movements, identifying trends, and making informed trading decisions. By using charts, indicators, and patterns, traders can develop strategies that capitalize on both market momentum and reversals, allowing them to maximize profits while managing risks.

As you progress through this book, you will delve deeper into the world of technical indicators and learn how to integrate them into your trading strategy effectively. The next chapter will introduce you to some of the most commonly used indicators, from moving averages to oscillators, and provide practical examples of how to apply them in real-world trading scenarios.

Chapter 2: Moving Averages

Introduction to Trend Indicators

Trend indicators are vital tools in the arsenal of any trader. They help in identifying and confirming the direction of market trends, which is essential for making informed trading decisions. By analyzing price data and smoothing out short-term fluctuations, trend indicators can provide a clearer picture of the market's overall direction. This chapter delves into some of the most commonly used trend indicators, including Moving Averages (MA), Exponential Moving Averages (EMA), and the Moving Average Convergence Divergence (MACD).

2.1: Moving Averages (MA)

Simple Moving Average (SMA

A Simple Moving Average (SMA) is a basic yet powerful trend indicator. It calculates the average of a selected range of prices, usually closing prices, by the number of periods in that range.

$$\text{SMA} = \frac{\sum_{i=1}^{n} P_i}{n}$$

Where:

- is the price at period .
- is the number of periods.

For instance, a 10-day SMA adds the closing prices of the last 10 days and divides by 10. This smooths out price data, making it easier to identify trends.

Application in Trading

SMAs are used to identify both long-term and short-term trends. A common strategy is to use two SMAs of different periods, such as the 50-day and 200-day SMAs. When the short-term SMA crosses above the long-term SMA, it signals a potential uptrend (a golden cross). Conversely, when the short-term SMA crosses below the long-term SMA, it indicates a potential downtrend (a death cross).

Interpretation

Interpreting SMA involves looking at crossovers and the slope of the SMA. A rising SMA indicates an uptrend, while a falling SMA suggests a downtrend.

Example of SMA Application

Golden Cross: The Golden Cross is a bullish signal that occurs when a short-term moving average crosses above a long-term moving average. Typically, the most common moving averages used are the 50-day and 200-day moving averages.

Significance

- **Bullish Indicator:** The Golden Cross indicates a potential upward trend, suggesting that a significant rally could be on the horizon.

- **Market Sentiment:** It reflects a shift in market sentiment from bearish to bullish, as short-term price movements are rising faster than long-term trends.

Example of Formation

- Short-Term Moving Average: Calculate the 50-day Simple Moving Average (SMA).

- Long-Term Moving Average: Calculate the 200-day SMA.

- Crossover: When the 50-day SMA crosses above the 200-day SMA, it forms a Golden Cross.

Application in Trading

- **Buy Signal:** Traders often interpret the Golden Cross as a signal to buy the asset, expecting further price appreciation.

- **Confirmation:** The strength of the Golden Cross can be confirmed by increasing trading volumes and other indicators like the MACD or RSI.

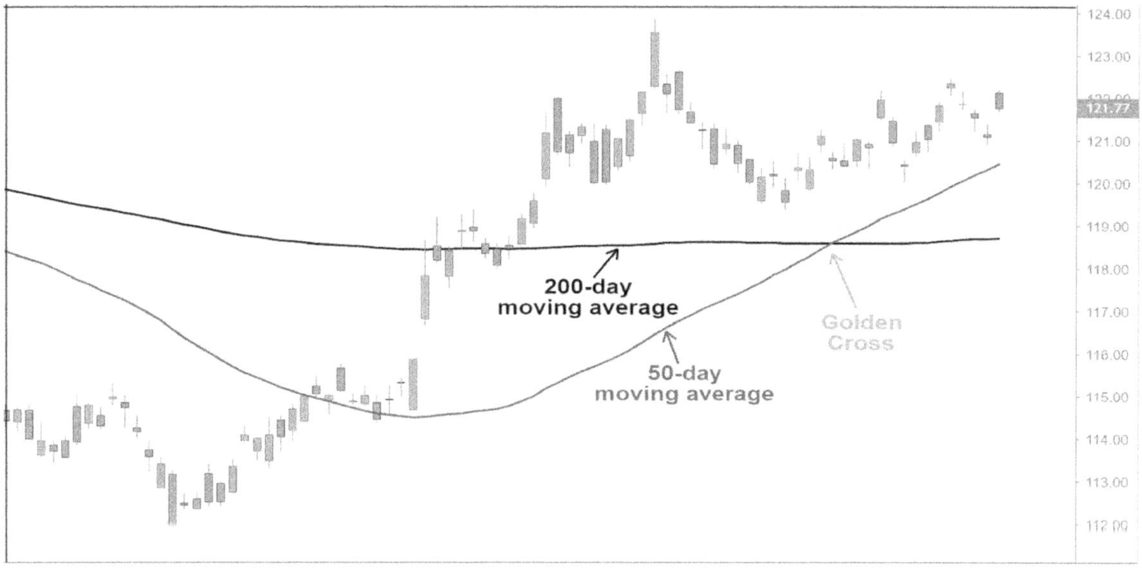

Death Cross: The Death Cross is a bearish signal that occurs when a short-term moving average crosses below a long-term moving average. The most common moving averages used are the 50-day and 200-day moving averages.

Significance

- **Bearish Indicator:** The Death Cross indicates a potential downward trend, suggesting that a significant sell-off could be impending.

- **Market Sentiment:** It reflects a shift in market sentiment from bullish to bearish, as short-term price movements are declining faster than long-term trends.

Example of Formation

- Short-Term Moving Average: Calculate the 50-day Simple Moving Average (SMA).

- Long-Term Moving Average: Calculate the 200-day SMA.

- Crossover: When the 50-day SMA crosses below the 200-day SMA, it forms a Death Cross.

Application in Trading

- **Sell Signal:** Traders often interpret the Death Cross as a signal to sell or short the asset, expecting further price depreciation.

Investopedia

- **Confirmation:** The strength of the Death Cross can be confirmed by increasing trading volumes and other indicators like the MACD or RSI.

Exponential Moving Average (EMA)

Explanation of Calculation

The Exponential Moving Average (EMA) gives more weight to recent prices, making it more responsive to new information. The EMA is calculated using the formula:

$$\text{EMA} = P_t \times k + \text{EMA}_{\text{previous}} \times (1 - k)$$

Where:

- is the price at time period

- is the smoothing constant, calculated as .

- is the EMA of the previous period.

Advantages in Volatile Markets

EMA's responsiveness to recent prices makes it particularly useful in volatile markets where quick trend reversals are common. It reacts faster to price changes than the SMA, providing traders with earlier signals.

Identifying Trend Reversals

The EMA is instrumental in identifying trend reversals. For instance, the 12-day and 26-day EMAs are often used together. When the 12-day EMA crosses above the 26-day EMA, it signals a bullish reversal, and when it crosses below, it signals a bearish reversal.

Example of EMA Application

Bullish Reversal: A Bullish Reversal with respect to EMA occurs when a shorter-period EMA crosses above a longer-period EMA, signaling a potential shift from a downtrend to an uptrend.

Significance

Indicator of Uptrend: This crossover suggests that recent price movements are gaining upward momentum.

Market Sentiment: It reflects a change in market sentiment from bearish to bullish.

Example of Identification

- **Short-Term EMA:** Calculate the 12-day EMA.
- **Long-Term EMA:** Calculate the 26-day EMA.
- **Crossover:** When the 12-day EMA crosses above the 26-day EMA, it signals a Bullish Reversal.

Application in Trading

- **Buy Signal:** Traders often interpret this crossover as a signal to buy the asset, anticipating further price increases.
- **Confirmation:** Traders may use other indicators like the Relative Strength Index (RSI) or Moving Average Convergence Divergence (MACD) to confirm the reversal.

Bearish Reversal: A Bearish Reversal with respect to EMA occurs when a shorter-period EMA crosses below a longer-period EMA, signaling a potential shift from an uptrend to a downtrend.

Significance

- **Indicator of Downtrend:** This crossover suggests that recent price movements are losing upward momentum and gaining downward momentum.
- **Market Sentiment:** It reflects a change in market sentiment from bullish to bearish.

Example of Identification

- **Short-Term EMA:** Calculate the 12-day EMA.
- **Long-Term EMA:** Calculate the 26-day EMA.
- **Crossover:** When the 12-day EMA crosses below the 26-day EMA, it signals a Bearish Reversal.

Application in Trading

- **Sell Signal:** Traders often interpret this crossover as a signal to sell or short the asset, anticipating further price decreases. Never buy just because the price is low, and never sell just because the price is high.
-
- **Confirmation:** Traders may use other indicators like the Relative Strength Index (RSI) or Moving Average Convergence Divergence (MACD) to confirm the reversal.

Practical Examples

Bullish Reversal Example

- Scenario: Imagine a stock in a downtrend where the 12-day EMA is below the 26-day EMA.
- Reversal Point: The stock begins to rise, and the 12-day EMA crosses above the 26-day EMA.

- Buy Signal: This crossover signals a potential Bullish Reversal, indicating an opportunity to buy the stock.

Bearish Reversal Example

- **Scenario:** Imagine a stock in an uptrend where the 12-day EMA is above the 26-day EMA.

- **Reversal Point:** The stock begins to fall, and the 12-day EMA crosses below the 26-day EMA.

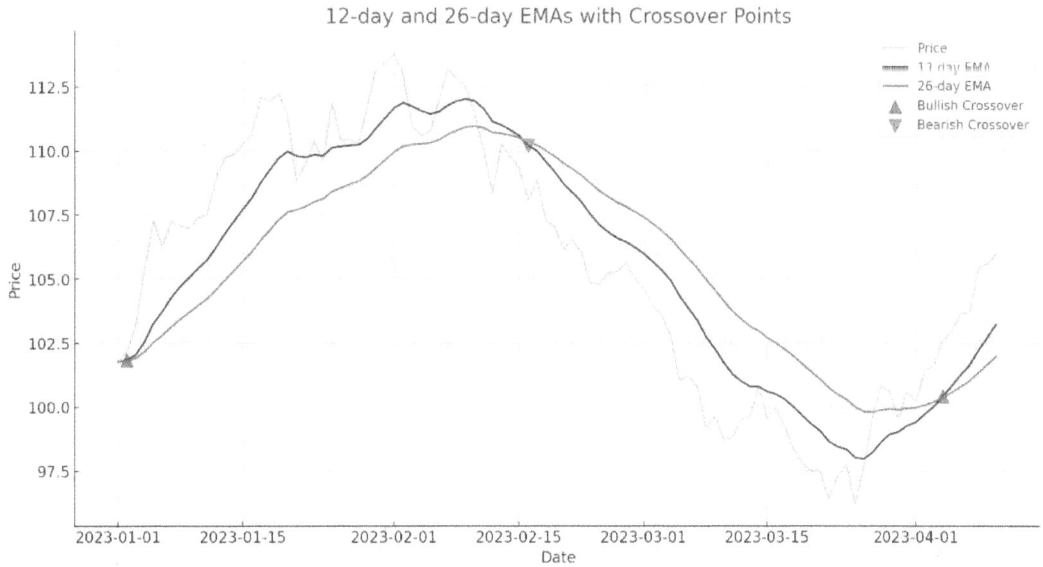

- **Sell Signal:** This crossover signals a potential Bearish Reversal, indicating an opportunity to sell or short the stock.

The chart shows the 12-day and 26-day EMAs with the points of crossover highlighted. The green upward-pointing triangles represent bullish crossovers, while the red downward-pointing triangles indicate bearish crossovers.

References

1. Murphy, J. J. (1999). Technical Analysis of the Financial Markets: A Comprehensive Guide to Trading Methods and Applications. New York Institute of Finance.

2. Pring, M. J. (2014). Technical Analysis Explained: The Successful Investor's Guide to Spotting Investment Trends and Turning Points. McGraw Hill Professional.

3. Wilder, J. W. (1978). New Concepts in Technical Trading Systems. Trend Research.

2.2: Moving Average Convergence Divergence (MACD)

Components of MACD

The MACD is a trend-following momentum indicator that shows the relationship between two moving averages of a security's price. It consists of three main components:

- **MACD Line:** The difference between the 12-day and 26-day EMAs.

- **Signal Line:** The 9-day EMA of the MACD line.

- **Histogram:** The difference between the MACD line and the signal line.

$$\text{MACD Line} = \text{EMA}_{12} - \text{EMA}_{26}$$
$$\text{Signal Line} = \text{EMA}_{9} \text{ of MACD Line}$$

Interpreting MACD

Bullish and Bearish Signals

- **Bullish Signal:** Occurs when the MACD line crosses above the signal line, indicating a potential upward movement.
- **Bearish Signal:** Occurs when the MACD line crosses below the signal line, indicating a potential downward movement.

Significance of MACD Histogram

The histogram represents the distance between the MACD line and the signal line. A positive histogram indicates that the MACD line is above the signal line, suggesting upward momentum. Conversely, a negative histogram indicates downward momentum.

Examples of MACD in Various Market Conditions

Bullish Crossover: A Bullish Crossover occurs when the MACD line crosses above the signal line. This event indicates that the upward momentum in the asset's price is increasing, suggesting a potential uptrend.

Significance

- **Indicator of Uptrend:** A Bullish Crossover signals that the asset's price may begin to rise, indicating a good time to enter a long position. "I'm not here for a long time, I'm here for a good time." - The Wolf of Wall Street (2013)

- **Market Sentiment:** It reflects a shift in market sentiment from bearish to bullish.

Example of Identification

- **Calculate the MACD Line:** Subtract the 26-day EMA from the 12-day EMA.

- **Calculate the Signal Line:** Compute the 9-day EMA of the MACD line.

- **Crossover Point:** When the MACD line crosses above the signal line, a Bullish Crossover is identified.

Application in Trading

- **Buy Signal:** Traders often interpret the Bullish Crossover as a signal to buy the asset, expecting further price appreciation.

- **Confirmation:** Additional indicators such as the Relative Strength Index (RSI) or volume analysis can be used to confirm the signal.

Bearish Crossover: A Bearish Crossover occurs when the MACD line crosses below the signal line. This event indicates that the downward momentum in the asset's price is increasing, suggesting a potential downtrend.

Significance

- **Indicator of Downtrend:** A Bearish Crossover signals that the asset's price may begin to fall, indicating a good time to enter a short position.

- **Market Sentiment:** It reflects a shift in market sentiment from bullish to bearish.

-

Example of Identification

- **Calculate the MACD Line:** Subtract the 26-day EMA from the 12-day EMA.
- **Calculate the Signal Line:** Compute the 9-day EMA of the MACD line.
- **Crossover Point:** When the MACD line crosses below the signal line, a Bearish Crossover is identified.

Application in Trading

- **Sell Signal:** Traders often interpret the Bearish Crossover as a signal to sell or short the asset, expecting further price depreciation.
- **Confirmation:** Additional indicators such as the Relative Strength Index (RSI) or volume analysis can be used to confirm the signal.

Practical Examples

Bullish Crossover Example

- **Scenario**: Imagine a stock that has been declining. The MACD line (difference between 12-day and 26-day EMA) starts to rise.
- **Crossover Point**: The MACD line crosses above the signal line (9-day EMA of MACD), indicating a Bullish Crossover.
- **Buy Signal**: This crossover signals a potential upward movement, indicating an opportunity to buy the stock.

Bearish Crossover Example

- **Scenario**: Imagine a stock that has been rising. The MACD line (difference between 12-day and 26-day EMA) starts to fall.
- **Crossover Point**: The MACD line crosses below the signal line (9-day EMA of MACD), indicating a Bearish Crossover.
- **Sell Signal**: This crossover signals a potential downward movement, indicating an opportunity to sell or short the stock.

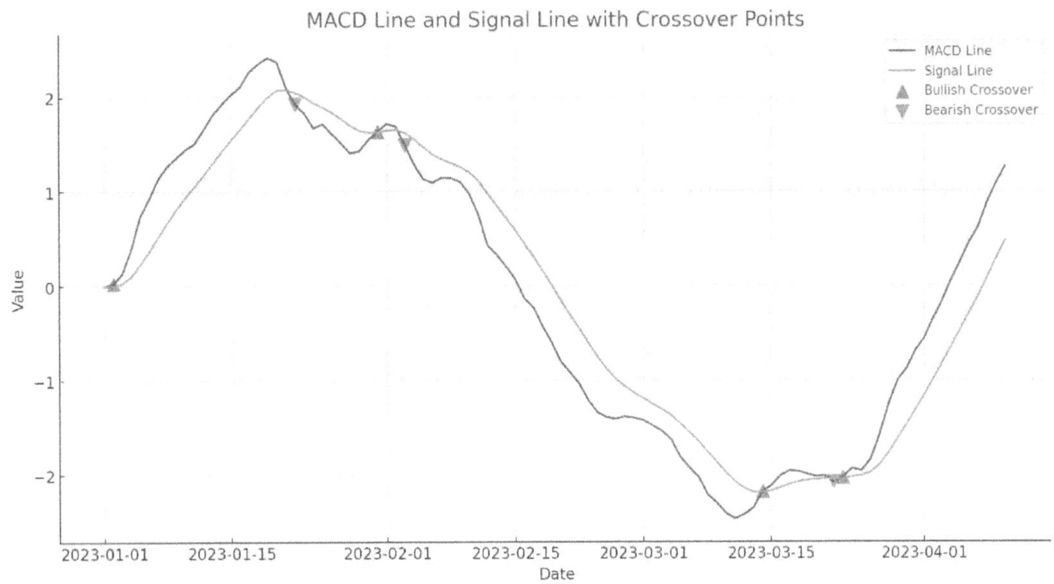

The chart shows the MACD line and the signal line with the points of crossover highlighted. The green upward-pointing triangles represent bullish crossovers, while the red downward-pointing triangles indicate bearish crossovers.

2.3: Bollinger Bands

Structure and Calculation

Bollinger Bands consist of three lines: the middle band and two outer bands. The middle band is typically a 20-day SMA, while the outer bands are set two standard deviations away from the middle band.

$$\text{Upper Band} = \text{SMA}_{20} + (2 \times \sigma)$$
$$\text{Lower Band} = \text{SMA}_{20} - (2 \times \sigma)$$

Where σ is the standard deviation of the price.

Applications in Trading

Detecting Volatility and Breakouts

- **Volatility:** The bands widen during periods of high volatility and contract during periods of low volatility.

- **Breakouts:** Prices touching or exceeding the bands can indicate potential breakouts. A breakout above the upper band suggests a bullish trend, while a breakout below the lower band suggests a bearish trend.

Identifying Overbought and Oversold Conditions

- **Overbought Condition:** Occurs when the price touches or moves above the upper band, indicating a potential sell signal.

- **Oversold Condition:** Occurs when the price touches or moves below the lower band, indicating a potential buy signal.

Case Studies of Bollinger Bands in Action

Case Study 1: Identifying Overbought Conditions

Scenario

A stock has been in a strong uptrend, and its price has repeatedly touched or exceeded the upper Bollinger Band.

Interpretation

When the price touches or moves above the upper band, it indicates that the stock may be overbought. This could signal a potential reversal or a pullback.

Example

- **Stock XYZ:** The stock price has been rising consistently for several weeks.

- **Bollinger Bands Analysis:** The price repeatedly touches the upper Bollinger Band, indicating overbought conditions.

- **Reversal Signal:** After touching the upper band, the stock price starts to consolidate and then decline.

Trading Strategy

- **Sell Signal:** Traders may consider selling the stock or taking profits when the price touches the upper band and shows signs of reversing.

- **Confirmation:** Additional indicators like the Relative Strength Index (RSI) can be used to confirm overbought conditions.

Case Study 2: Identifying Oversold Conditions

Scenario

A stock has been in a prolonged downtrend, and its price has repeatedly touched or fallen below the lower Bollinger Band.

Interpretation

When the price touches or falls below the lower band, it indicates that the stock may be oversold. This could signal a potential reversal or a bounce.

Example

- **Stock ABC:** The stock price has been declining for several weeks.
- **Bollinger Bands Analysis:** The price repeatedly touches the lower Bollinger Band, indicating oversold conditions.
- **Reversal Signal:** After touching the lower band, the stock price starts to stabilize and then rise.

Trading Strategy

- **Buy Signal:** Traders may consider buying the stock when the price touches the lower band and shows signs of reversing.
- **Confirmation:** Additional indicators like the Relative Strength Index (RSI) can be used to confirm oversold conditions.

Case Study 3: Detecting Volatility and Potential Breakouts

Scenario

A stock has been trading in a narrow range with low volatility, as indicated by the contraction of Bollinger Bands. Suddenly, the price breaks out of the range, and the bands widen.

Interpretation

When Bollinger Bands contract, it indicates low volatility and potential consolidation. A breakout above or below the bands suggests a significant move in that direction.

Example

- **Stock DEF:** The stock price has been moving sideways within a narrow range.
- **Bollinger Bands Analysis:** The bands contract, indicating low volatility.
- **Breakout Signal:** The price breaks above the upper band with increased volume, suggesting a bullish breakout.

Trading Strategy

- **Buy Signal:** Traders may consider buying the stock when it breaks above the upper band with strong volume.
- **Sell Signal:** Conversely, a breakout below the lower band with strong volume could signal a bearish breakout and a potential sell opportunity.

Case Study 4: Bollinger Band Squeeze

Scenario

A stock's Bollinger Bands have narrowed significantly, indicating a period of low volatility. This is often a precursor to a significant price movement.

Interpretation

A Bollinger Band Squeeze occurs when the bands come close together. This usually precedes a period of high volatility and significant price movement in either direction.

Example

- **Stock GHI:** The stock price has been trading in a tight range, and the Bollinger Bands have squeezed.
- **Bollinger Bands Analysis:** The bands are very close together, indicating low volatility.

- **Breakout Signal:** The price breaks out above the upper band, initiating a strong upward trend.

Trading Strategy

- **Buy Signal:** Traders may consider buying the stock when it breaks out above the squeezed bands with high volume.

- **Sell Signal:** A breakout below the squeezed bands with high volume could signal a potential sell opportunity.

Summary

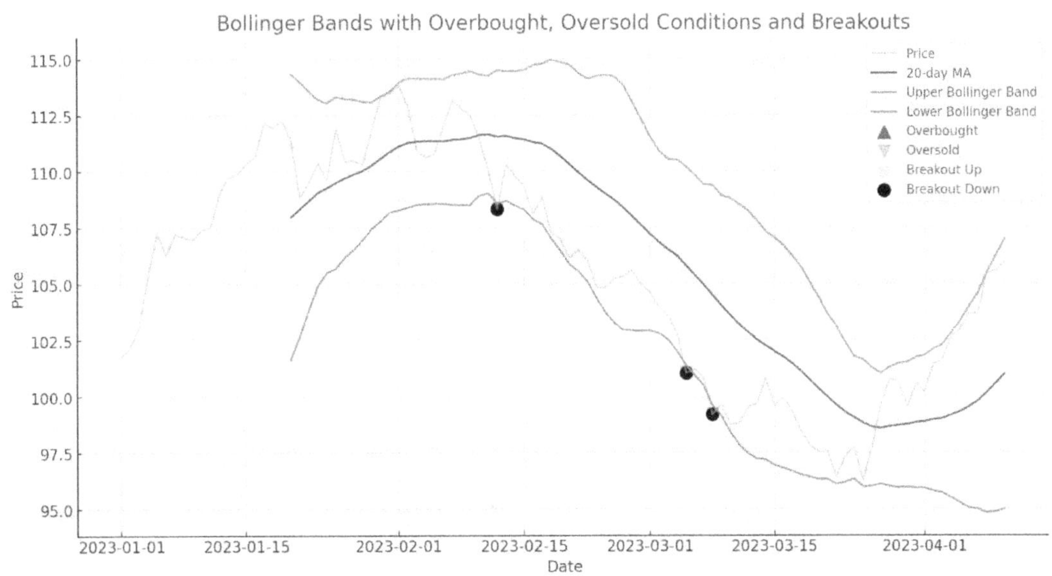

Bollinger Bands are versatile tools that help traders identify overbought and oversold conditions, detect volatility, and anticipate potential breakouts. By analyzing the relationship between price and Bollinger Bands, traders can make informed decisions and develop effective trading strategies.

The chart shows Bollinger Bands with examples of overbought and oversold conditions as well as breakouts. The purple upward-pointing triangles represent overbought conditions, the orange downward-pointing triangles indicate oversold conditions, the gold circles represent breakout up, and the black circles indicate breakout down.

The Pitfalls of Curve-Fitted Trading Programs

While the allure of a curve-fitted trading program can be strong, especially when backtesting yields seemingly spectacular results, these programs are fraught with significant risks. Understanding the limitations and dangers of curve fitting is crucial for any trader looking to build a sustainable and profitable trading strategy.

1. Poor Generalization and Market Adaptation: Curve-fitted programs excel at replicating past market behaviors but often falter when confronted with new or changing market conditions. This shortfall stems from their design, which optimizes for specific noise and patterns in historical data rather than capturing the underlying market dynamics. As a result, these programs may perform well in backtests but struggle to adapt when the market shifts, leading to inconsistent results or significant losses.

2. The Trap of Over-Optimization: In the pursuit of perfect historical performance, curve fitting frequently involves adding numerous parameters or rules to a trading strategy. While this may enhance backtest results, it often creates a complex and inflexible program. This over-optimization can lead to overfitting, where the program is so tailored to the historical data that it becomes sensitive to minor market fluctuations, which are unlikely to recur in the future.

3. False Sense of Security and Unrealistic Expectations: The impressive results of a curve-fitted program during backtesting can create a false sense of security for the trader. However, these results are often misleading, as they do not guarantee future success. This false confidence can lead to unrealistic expectations about the program's profitability, causing traders to make impulsive or risky decisions. The reality is that market conditions are ever-changing, and a strategy that worked in the past may not perform well in the future.

4. Difficulty in Adaptation and Risk of Significant Losses: When market conditions change—such as shifts in volatility, trends, or market sentiment—a curve-fitted trading program may struggle to adapt. This lack of adaptability can lead to significant losses, as the program is unable to adjust its strategies to the new market environment. For traders, this can result in frustration and a loss of confidence in their trading systems.

5. The Importance of Robust Trading Programs: In contrast to curve-fitted programs, robust trading programs are designed to perform consistently across a wide range of market conditions. These programs are built with flexibility and resilience, ensuring that their performance is not significantly degraded when faced with unforeseen market changes. Developing a robust trading program involves rigorous testing across multiple datasets and market conditions, including out-of-sample testing and stress-testing under various scenarios. This approach reduces the risk of overfitting and increases the likelihood of long-term profitability.

Key Risks in Technical Trading and Their Mitigation

Technical trading, while offering the potential for substantial profits, presents unique challenges that traders must navigate to achieve consistent success. Understanding these risks and employing effective mitigation strategies is essential for thriving in the dynamic world of financial markets.

1. False Signals and Whipsaws: Technical indicators and chart patterns, though powerful tools, are not infallible. They can produce false signals, especially in volatile or range-bound markets, leading to what is known as a whipsaw—where a trader enters a trade based on a signal only for the market to reverse direction abruptly. Relying on a single indicator or failing to seek confirmation from multiple sources can lead to significant losses. Trade only when the market is bullish or bearish.

Mitigation Strategy: Multi-Indicator Confirmation To mitigate the risk of false signals, traders should avoid relying on a single indicator. Instead, combine multiple indicators or analysis methods to confirm signals and filter out false positives. For example, pairing a 34-day EMA with the MACD, RSI, or other momentum indicators can provide a more comprehensive assessment of market conditions and reduce the likelihood of falling victim to whipsaws.

2. Over-Reliance on Indicators: While technical analysis is a valuable tool, it should not be the sole determinant of market behavior. Relying exclusively on technical indicators without considering fundamental factors or market sentiment can lead to misinterpretations and misguided trades.

Mitigation Strategy: Fundamental Analysis Integration Incorporate fundamental analysis to supplement your technical approach. Understanding the underlying factors influencing a company or market can provide valuable context for interpreting technical signals and making more informed decisions. By combining technical and fundamental analysis, traders can develop a more holistic view of the market.

3. Emotional Trading Pitfalls: Emotions like fear and greed are powerful forces that can drive irrational decision-making in trading. The fear of missing out (FOMO) can lead to impulsive entries, while the fear of losses can cause premature exits. Maintaining emotional discipline is essential for executing a trading plan effectively.

Mitigation Strategy: Emotional Intelligence and Discipline Developing emotional resilience and discipline is crucial to avoid impulsive trading decisions. Stick to your pre-defined trading plan, manage risk effectively, and resist the urge to chase quick profits or recover losses hastily. By controlling emotions and adhering to a strategy, traders can navigate the market more effectively and avoid costly mistakes.

4. Lack of Discipline and Deviation from the Plan: A well-defined trading plan serves as a roadmap through the market's complexities. However, traders often deviate from this plan due to impatience, overconfidence, or external pressures, which can derail even the most promising strategies.

Mitigation Strategy: Adherence to a Trading Plan Discipline is the cornerstone of successful trading. Traders must adhere to their trading plans, which should include clearly defined entry and exit points, risk management protocols, and criteria for trade evaluation. By following a plan consistently, traders can avoid impulsive decisions and stay on course toward their trading goals.

5. Data Limitations and Historical Analysis: Technical analysis relies heavily on historical data, but past performance does not guarantee future results. Market conditions can change rapidly, rendering historical patterns irrelevant or misleading.

Mitigation Strategy: Continuous Learning and Adaptation Markets evolve, and so should a trader's knowledge and strategies. Stay abreast of emerging trends, new indicators, and alternative analysis methods. By continuously learning and adapting strategies to remain effective in changing market conditions, traders can improve their chances of success.

Mean Reversion: Theory and Application in Trading

Mean reversion is a financial theory suggesting that asset prices and historical returns eventually revert to their long-term average or mean over time. This concept is foundational to various trading strategies, particularly in range-bound or sideways markets where prices oscillate within a specific range.

Key Points about Mean Reversion:

- **Foundation:** The theory is based on the idea that market fluctuations are often temporary, and prices tend to stabilize around their average over the long run.
- **Application:** It is used as the basis for various trading strategies across different asset classes, including stocks, currencies, and commodities.

- **Indicators:** Investors often use technical indicators like moving averages, RSI, and Bollinger Bands to identify mean-reverting opportunities.

- **Timeframes:** Mean reversion strategies can be applied across different periods, from short-term (intraday) to long-term investing.

- **Effectiveness:** Mean reversion strategies are most effective in range-bound or sideways markets, where prices oscillate within a specific range.

How Investors Use Mean Reversion:

- **Identifying Overvalued/Undervalued Assets:** Investors look for assets that have deviated significantly from their historical average. If an asset is overvalued, they might consider selling or shorting it, expecting the price to fall back to the mean. Conversely, if an asset is undervalued, they might consider buying it, anticipating the price to rise.

- **Entry and Exit Points:** Mean reversion indicators can help investors determine potential entry and exit points for their trades. For example, if an asset's price has fallen below its moving average, it could signal a buying opportunity, anticipating a rebound.

- **Risk Management:** Mean reversion strategies can also be used for risk management. For instance, if a portfolio of stocks has experienced a significant increase in value, an investor might consider rebalancing by selling some overvalued stocks and buying undervalued ones to bring the portfolio back in line with its long-term average. Be a long-term investor, not a short-term trader.

Common Mean Reversion Strategies and Indicators:

- **Pairs Trading:** This strategy involves identifying pairs of stocks that historically move together. When one stock deviates from the other, a trader buys the underperforming stock and sells the outperforming one, betting that their prices will converge again.

- **RSI (Relative Strength Index) Reversal:** The RSI measures the magnitude of recent price changes to evaluate overbought or oversold conditions. A reading above 70 typically suggests an overbought asset, while a reading below 30 suggests an oversold asset. Traders might enter a short position when the RSI is above 70 and a long position when it's below 30, anticipating a reversal to the mean.

- **Bollinger Band Bounce:** Bollinger Bands consist of a middle band (typically a moving average) and two outer bands representing standard deviations from the middle band. When the price touches or crosses an outer band, traders might anticipate a bounce back toward the middle band, representing a reversion to the mean.

- **Moving Average Crossover:** This strategy involves using two moving averages (e.g., a short-term 50-day moving average and a long-term 200-day moving average). When the short-term moving average crosses above the long-term moving average, it signals a potential uptrend and a buying opportunity. Conversely, a cross below signals a potential downtrend and a selling opportunity.

Limitations and Best Practices for Using Mean Reversion:

- **Market Trends:** Mean reversion strategies may be less effective in strongly trending markets, where prices continue to move in one direction without reverting to the mean. In such scenarios, traders might need to consider trend-following strategies.

- **Timeframe Consideration:** The effectiveness of mean reversion can vary depending on the timeframe. Short-term traders might focus on intraday reversions, while long-term investors may look at multi-year averages.

- **Indicator Sensitivity:** The choice of mean reversion indicators and their settings (e.g., period length) can significantly impact the strategy's effectiveness. Traders should backtest different settings and choose those that align with their trading goals and market conditions.

- **Adaptation to Market Conditions:** Mean reversion strategies should be adapted to current market conditions. For instance, during periods of high volatility, traders might use wider bands or longer moving averages to account for larger price swings.

References

1. Murphy, J. J. (1999). Technical Analysis of the Financial Markets: A Comprehensive Guide to Trading Methods and Applications. New York Institute of Finance.

2. Pring, M. J. (2014). Technical Analysis Explained: The Successful Investor's Guide to Spotting Investment Trends and Turning Points. McGraw Hill Professional.

3. Wilder, J. W. (1978). New Concepts in Technical Trading Systems. Trend Research.

4. Bollinger, J. (2001). Bollinger on Bollinger Bands. McGraw Hill Professional.

Chapter 3: Bollinger Bands

History and Development of Bollinger Bands

The development of Bollinger Bands dates back to the early 1980s, a period marked by significant advances in technical analysis tools. John Bollinger, a seasoned market technician, sought a more adaptable and dynamic tool to assess market volatility and identify trading opportunities. Bollinger Bands emerged as a response to the limitations of existing methods, such as simple moving averages and traditional support and resistance levels, which often failed to account for changing market conditions.

Bollinger was inspired by earlier work on moving averages and standard deviations—two concepts central to statistical analysis. He innovatively combined these elements to create a tool that not only tracks price movement but also adjusts to volatility. The middle line of Bollinger Bands represents a simple moving average (SMA), typically over 20 periods, while the upper and lower bands are placed two standard deviations away from the SMA. This configuration allows the bands to expand and contract based on market volatility, making them more responsive to changing conditions than static indicators.

Initially, Bollinger Bands gained popularity among stock traders due to their effectiveness in identifying overbought and oversold conditions. Over time, the tool's utility extended to various asset classes, including forex, commodities, and, more recently, cryptocurrencies. The adaptability of Bollinger Bands has made them a staple in the toolkit of traders across diverse markets. Their continued relevance in modern trading speaks to the robustness of Bollinger's original design.

Components of Bollinger Bands

Bollinger Bands are a powerful technical analysis tool developed by John Bollinger in the 1980s. They consist of three primary components: the middle line, which is usually a Simple Moving Average (SMA) or an Exponential Moving Average (EMA), and the upper and lower bands that are calculated based on standard deviations from the middle line. This structure allows traders to assess market volatility and identify potential reversal points, making Bollinger Bands an essential tool in the arsenal of any technical analyst.

Middle Line (SMA or EMA)

The middle line of the Bollinger Bands is typically a 20-day SMA or EMA, which serves as the basis for calculating the upper and lower bands. The choice between SMA and EMA depends on the trader's preference and the specific characteristics of the market being analyzed.

- **Simple Moving Average (SMA):** The SMA is calculated by taking the arithmetic mean of a set of prices over a specified period. For example, in a 20-day SMA, the closing prices of the last 20 days are summed and then divided by 20. The SMA is a lagging indicator, which means it reflects past price movements and may not respond quickly to rapid price changes.

- **Exponential Moving Average (EMA):** The EMA gives more weight to recent prices, making it more responsive to current market conditions compared to the SMA. The calculation of EMA involves applying a multiplier to the most recent price, with the weighting decreasing exponentially for each preceding price point. This characteristic makes the EMA more suitable for markets that are prone to sharp movements and volatility.

The middle line acts as a trend indicator, with prices generally oscillating above and below it. When prices consistently stay above the middle line, it indicates an uptrend, while prices staying below the middle line suggest a downtrend.

Upper and Lower Bands

The upper and lower bands are constructed by adding and subtracting a standard deviation value from the middle line. Standard deviation measures the dispersion of data points from their mean and is used in Bollinger Bands to reflect market volatility.

- **Calculation of Bands:** For a 20-day Bollinger Band with two standard deviations (the most common setting), the upper band is calculated by adding two standard deviations to the 20-day SMA, while the lower band is calculated by subtracting two standard deviations from the 20-day SMA.

Upper Band=SMA20+(2×σ20)\text{Upper Band} = SMA_{20} + (2 \times \sigma_{20})Upper Band=SMA20+(2×σ20) Lower Band=SMA20−(2×σ20)\text{Lower Band} = SMA_{20} - (2 \times \sigma_{20})Lower Band=SMA20−(2×σ20)

Where σ20\sigma_{20}σ20 is the 20-day standard deviation of the asset's price.

- **Volatility and Band Width:** The distance between the upper and lower bands, known as the band width, expands and contracts in response to market volatility. During periods of high volatility, the bands widen, signaling that prices are moving away from the average at a faster pace. Conversely, during low volatility, the bands contract, indicating that prices are staying close to the average.

The dynamic nature of Bollinger Bands makes them a versatile tool for analyzing market conditions. Traders often use the bands not only to assess volatility but also to identify potential price breakouts, reversals, and continuation patterns.

Using Bollinger Bands for Volatility Assessment and Trend Reversals

Bollinger Bands are highly effective for assessing market volatility and identifying potential trend reversals. By analyzing the relationship between price and the bands, traders can gain insights into the market's current state and anticipate future movements.

Volatility Assessment

- **Squeeze:** The "Bollinger Squeeze" occurs when the bands contract significantly, indicating a period of low volatility. This contraction often precedes a sharp price movement, as the market builds up pressure that eventually leads to a breakout. The squeeze is a critical signal for traders, as it alerts them to the possibility of an impending price move, though the direction of the move is not always predictable.

- **Breakout Signals:** When prices break above the upper band or below the lower band after a squeeze, it often signals the beginning of a new trend. A breakout above the upper band suggests a potential uptrend, while a breakout below the lower band indicates a possible downtrend. However, traders should be cautious, as false breakouts can occur, leading to premature entries or exits.

- **Trend Confirmation:** The movement of prices relative to the bands can also confirm the strength of a trend. In a strong uptrend, prices will often "ride the band," staying close to the upper band without crossing below the middle line. Conversely, in a strong downtrend, prices will hug the lower band, with limited movement above the middle line. This "walking the band" behavior is a key indicator of trend persistence.

Identifying Trend Reversals

- **Overbought and Oversold Conditions:** Bollinger Bands can help identify overbought and oversold conditions, which often precede trend reversals. When prices touch or move beyond the upper band, it may indicate that the asset is overbought, signaling a potential downward correction. Similarly, when prices touch or drop below the lower band, it may suggest that the asset is oversold, pointing to a possible upward reversal.

- **Double Tops and Bottoms:** Bollinger Bands can be used in conjunction with chart patterns like double tops and bottoms to identify reversal points. A double top is formed when prices reach the upper band twice with a small dip in between, suggesting that the uptrend may be losing momentum. A double bottom occurs when prices hit the lower band twice with a brief rally in between, indicating that the downtrend may be coming to an end.

- **Divergence:** Divergence between price movement and the Bollinger Bands can also signal a reversal. For example, if prices make a new high that touches the upper band, but the band does not make a corresponding new high, it could indicate that the uptrend is weakening and a reversal may be imminent.

Practical Applications and Trading Strategies

Bollinger Bands offer a wide range of practical applications for traders. By integrating them into various trading strategies, traders can enhance their decision-making process and improve their chances of success in the market.

1. Bollinger Band Bounce

The Bollinger Band Bounce strategy is based on the idea that prices tend to revert to the mean, or the middle line, after reaching the upper or lower bands. This mean reversion strategy is particularly effective in range-bound markets where prices oscillate within a well-defined range.

- **Entry and Exit Points:** Traders using this strategy typically enter a trade when prices touch the lower band (buy signal) or the upper band (sell signal), anticipating a reversal towards the middle line. They exit the trade once prices reach the middle line or when the opposite band is touched.

- **Confirmation Tools:** To increase the reliability of this strategy, traders often use additional confirmation tools such as Relative Strength Index (RSI) or Moving Average Convergence Divergence (MACD) to assess whether the market is truly overbought or oversold.

2. Bollinger Band Breakout

The Bollinger Band Breakout strategy capitalizes on the strong price movements that follow a period of low volatility. When the bands squeeze tightly together, traders prepare for a potential breakout, which could signal the start of a new trend.

- **Identifying Breakouts:** Traders look for prices to close above the upper band (buy signal) or below the lower band (sell signal) following a squeeze. This breakout is often accompanied by increased volume, further confirming the strength of the move.

- **Risk Management:** Since breakouts can sometimes be false, it's crucial to set stop-loss orders just below the middle line in the case of an upward breakout or just above the middle line for a downward breakout. This helps protect against unexpected reversals.

3. Bollinger Band and RSI Combo

Combining Bollinger Bands with the RSI can create a powerful trading system that filters out false signals and enhances trend identification.

- **RSI as a Confirmation Tool:** When prices touch the upper band and the RSI is in the overbought zone (typically above 70), it strengthens the case for a potential reversal. Conversely, when prices touch the lower band and the RSI is in the oversold zone (typically below 30), it increases the likelihood of an upward reversal.

- **Trade Setup:** Traders enter a sell position when prices hit the upper band, and the RSI confirms overbought conditions. They enter a buy position when prices reach the lower band, and the RSI confirms oversold conditions.

4. Bollinger Band and MACD Strategy

The Moving Average Convergence Divergence (MACD) indicator complements Bollinger Bands by providing insights into momentum and trend direction.

- **Identifying Trends:** When the MACD line crosses above the signal line, it indicates bullish momentum, which can be further validated if prices are near the lower band, suggesting a potential upward reversal. Conversely, when the MACD line crosses below the signal line, it signals bearish momentum, which can be confirmed if prices are near the upper band.

- **Entry and Exit Points:** Traders can enter long positions when the MACD line crosses above the signal line, and prices are near the lower band. They can enter short positions when the MACD line crosses below the signal line, and prices are near the upper band. Exiting the trade can be done when the opposite band is approached or when the MACD gives a contrary signal.

5. Bollinger Bands in Trend Following

Bollinger Bands are not only useful for identifying reversals but also for following trends. In a trending market, prices often "walk the band," meaning they consistently stay near one of the bands without reverting to the middle line.

- **Trend Continuation:** Traders using Bollinger Bands in a trend-following strategy focus on entering positions in the direction of the trend when prices are near the band. For example, in an uptrend, they would look for buying opportunities when prices touch the middle line after pulling back from the upper band.

- **Adjusting Band Parameters:** To better suit trend-following, traders might adjust the band parameters, such as using a longer period for the SMA (e.g., 50-day) or increasing the number of standard deviations to reduce the frequency of signals and focus on more significant moves.

6. Backtesting and Performance Analysis

Backtesting is an essential step in developing and refining trading strategies involving Bollinger Bands. Backtesting involves applying a trading strategy to historical price data to evaluate its performance over time. This process allows traders to understand the potential risks and rewards of their strategies before applying them in live markets.

For Bollinger Band strategies, backtesting can help identify the most effective parameters, such as the period length for the moving average and the standard deviation multiplier. It also reveals how the strategy performs under different market conditions—whether it thrives in trending markets, struggles in sideways markets, or excels during periods of high volatility.

For example, a trader might backtest a Bollinger Band Bounce strategy, where they buy when the price touches the lower band and sell when it reaches the middle band or the upper band. The backtest would reveal how this strategy performs over a range of historical periods and market conditions, providing data on win rates, average returns, and drawdowns. If the backtest shows consistent profitability with manageable risk, the trader can have more confidence in using the strategy moving forward.

Moreover, performance analysis from backtesting can highlight potential areas for improvement. Traders might discover that adjusting the band settings or combining Bollinger Bands with other indicators like RSI or MACD improves the strategy's effectiveness. Continuous backtesting and optimization are key to adapting Bollinger Band strategies to changing market environments.

Advanced Techniques and Considerations

While Bollinger Bands are straightforward to use, advanced traders often refine their approach by incorporating additional techniques and considerations.

While the standard setting for Bollinger Bands is a 20-day simple moving average (SMA) with bands set at two standard deviations, experienced traders often customize these parameters to better suit their specific trading style or the characteristics of the market they are analyzing. This customization is crucial because different markets and trading strategies can exhibit varying levels of volatility and price behavior, making the default settings less optimal in certain scenarios.

For example, in markets that exhibit higher volatility, such as cryptocurrency trading, traders might opt for a shorter period for the SMA, such as 10 days, to make the bands more responsive to rapid price changes. Similarly, reducing the standard deviation multiplier to 1.5 or even 1.0 can make the bands narrower, increasing the frequency of signals but also the potential for false positives.

On the other hand, in more stable markets like large-cap stocks or bonds, traders might prefer a longer period, such as a 50-day SMA, and widen the bands to three standard deviations. This adjustment reduces the frequency of signals, focusing on more significant price movements that are less likely to be noise. This approach is particularly useful for long-term investors who are more interested in capturing major trends rather than short-term fluctuations.

Additionally, some traders experiment with exponential moving averages (EMA) instead of SMAs for the middle line. The EMA gives more weight to recent prices, making it more responsive to current market conditions, which can be advantageous in fast-moving markets.

These alternative settings allow traders to tailor Bollinger Bands to their specific needs, enhancing their effectiveness across different trading environments. The key is to understand the nature of the market or asset being traded and adjust the Bollinger Bands' settings accordingly to optimize performance.

Bollinger Bands in Algorithmic Trading

In the era of high-frequency trading and complex algorithms, Bollinger Bands have found a new application in the realm of algorithmic trading. Algorithmic trading involves using computer programs to execute trades based on predefined criteria, such as technical indicators, price patterns, or market conditions. Bollinger Bands, with their mathematical precision and adaptability, are particularly well-suited for integration into these automated systems.

Traders and quants can program algorithms to automatically execute buy or sell orders when specific conditions related to Bollinger Bands are met. For example, an algorithm might be designed to initiate a buy order when the price touches the lower Bollinger Band and a sell order when the price hits the upper band. Such a system could be further enhanced by incorporating rules for volatility filtering, ensuring that trades are only executed when market conditions meet certain thresholds.

Additionally, algorithms can dynamically adjust Bollinger Band settings in real time based on current market volatility. For instance, in periods of low volatility, the algorithm might narrow the bands to capture more frequent trading opportunities, while in high-volatility environments, it could widen the bands to avoid whipsaws and false signals. This adaptability allows the algorithm to maintain effectiveness across different market conditions, enhancing its robustness.

The use of Bollinger Bands in algorithmic trading also enables backtesting on a larger scale. Algorithms can be backtested on extensive datasets, spanning multiple years and including a wide range of market conditions. This large-scale testing provides deep insights into the strategy's long-term performance, including its strengths, weaknesses, and potential areas for optimization.

However, the automation of Bollinger Band strategies is not without challenges. The risk of overfitting—where an algorithm is too closely tailored to historical data—can lead to poor performance in live markets. Therefore, continuous monitoring and adjustment of the algorithm are necessary to ensure it remains effective.

In summary, the integration of Bollinger Bands into algorithmic trading systems represents a powerful fusion of traditional technical analysis with modern technology. This approach appeals to traders who value efficiency, precision, and the ability to manage large volumes of trades in a systematic manner.

Multi-Time Frame Analysis

Using Bollinger Bands across multiple time frames can provide a more comprehensive view of the market. For example, a trader might use Bollinger Bands on a daily chart to identify the overall trend and then switch to an hourly chart to time their entry and exit points more precisely.

- **Higher Time Frame for Trend Identification:** The higher time frame (e.g., daily or weekly) helps identify the broader trend, which guides the trader's bias (bullish or bearish). The lower time frame (e.g., hourly or 15-minute) is then used for spotting entry points that align with the broader trend.

- **Combining Signals:** A trader might look for a squeeze on the higher time frame, indicating an impending breakout, and then monitor the lower time frame for a breakout confirmation, allowing for more precise timing.

Customizing Bollinger Bands

Traders can customize the parameters of Bollinger Bands to suit their specific trading style and the market they are analyzing.

- **Changing the Period Length:** Adjusting the period length of the SMA or EMA can make Bollinger Bands more or less sensitive to price movements. For instance, a shorter period (e.g., 10 days) will make the bands more responsive to recent price changes, while a longer period (e.g., 50 days) will smooth out short-term fluctuations.

- **Adjusting the Standard Deviation:** While two standard deviations are commonly used, traders may experiment with different settings. For example, using 1.5 standard deviations will narrow the bands, making them more sensitive to price changes, while using 2.5 standard deviations will widen the bands, reducing the frequency of signals but potentially increasing their reliability.

Bollinger Bands with Other Indicators

Incorporating other technical indicators can enhance the effectiveness of Bollinger Bands.

- **Volume Analysis:** Volume is a critical factor in confirming Bollinger Band signals. For instance, a breakout that occurs on high volume is more likely to lead to a sustained trend than one that occurs on low volume. Traders can use volume indicators such as On-

Balance Volume (OBV) or the Volume-Weighted Average Price (VWAP) alongside Bollinger Bands.

- **Fibonacci Retracements:** Combining Bollinger Bands with Fibonacci retracement levels can help identify key support and resistance areas. For example, if a price touches the lower band at a 61.8% Fibonacci retracement level, it may indicate a strong potential for a reversal.

Psychological and Emotional Aspects

Successful trading with Bollinger Bands also involves managing psychological and emotional factors. Traders must avoid the temptation to act impulsively when prices touch the bands and instead rely on a disciplined approach that includes confirmation from other indicators or patterns.

- **Patience and Discipline:** Bollinger Bands require traders to be patient and wait for the right setup. Entering a trade too early or without proper confirmation can lead to losses. Sticking to a well-defined trading plan and maintaining discipline is crucial. Be patient. Be disciplined.

- **Managing Emotions:** Emotional reactions to market movements can lead to poor decision-making. Traders should remain calm and focused, using Bollinger Bands as part of a comprehensive strategy rather than a standalone tool.

Empirical Studies on the Effectiveness of Bollinger Bands

The effectiveness of Bollinger Bands has been the subject of extensive empirical research, reflecting their widespread use in the trading community. A notable study by Lento, Gradojevic, and Wright (2007) explored the application of Bollinger Bands across various market conditions. Their research demonstrated that Bollinger Bands, particularly when used in conjunction with other technical indicators like the Relative Strength Index (RSI), can significantly enhance trading performance. The combination of Bollinger Bands with RSI was found to be effective in identifying market turning points, thereby improving the accuracy of trade entries and exits.

Another important study by Wang and Huang (2012) focused on the performance of Bollinger Bands in trending versus sideways markets. They found that Bollinger Bands are particularly effective in trending markets, where the price tends to 'ride the bands,' signaling a strong continuation of the trend. In contrast, the bands' effectiveness diminishes in sideways or range-bound markets, where frequent false signals can occur due to the lack of a clear trend direction.

These studies provide a data-driven foundation for the use of Bollinger Bands in trading. They validate the tool's utility in various market conditions and underscore the importance of combining Bollinger Bands with other indicators to filter out false signals and enhance decision-making. The empirical evidence suggests that while Bollinger Bands are powerful, their effectiveness is maximized when used as part of a broader strategy that includes other technical and fundamental analyses.

Bollinger Bands and Market Sentiment

Bollinger Bands are not just a tool for assessing volatility; they can also provide valuable insights into market sentiment, which is a critical driver of price action. Market sentiment refers to the overall attitude of investors towards a particular security or the market as a whole. It can be bullish, bearish, or neutral, and it often influences trading behavior, sometimes more so than fundamental factors.

When prices consistently hover near the upper Bollinger Band, it is often an indication of bullish sentiment, suggesting that buyers are in control and that the market may continue to rise. This scenario is particularly significant when accompanied by strong volume, as it indicates broad market participation in the uptrend. Conversely, when prices remain close to the lower Bollinger Band, it signals bearish sentiment, with sellers dominating the market and pushing prices down.

Bollinger Bands can also highlight extremes in market sentiment. For example, if prices break above the upper band after a prolonged uptrend, it might indicate that the market is becoming overbought, with excessively bullish sentiment potentially leading to a correction. Similarly, if prices drop below the lower band after a sustained downtrend, it may suggest that the market is oversold, and a reversal could be imminent as bearish sentiment peaks. Wait for the market to confirm your opinion.

Understanding market sentiment through Bollinger Bands allows traders to anticipate potential reversals or continuations in price trends. By combining this insight with other technical and fundamental indicators, traders can better navigate the emotional highs and lows of the market, making more informed and less impulsive decisions.

Case Studies and Historical Examples

Examining historical examples of Bollinger Band usage can provide valuable insights into their practical application.

1. The 2008 Financial Crisis

During the 2008 financial crisis, Bollinger Bands played a critical role in helping traders navigate extreme market volatility.

- **S&P 500 Analysis:** In the months leading up to the crisis, the S&P 500 experienced several Bollinger Squeezes, followed by sharp breakouts to the downside. Traders who recognized these patterns and used them in conjunction with other indicators, such as RSI and MACD, were able to identify the early stages of the market collapse and take protective measures.

- **Gold Prices:** Gold prices, often considered a safe haven during times of economic uncertainty, also exhibited significant Bollinger Band activity during the crisis. As equity markets plummeted, gold prices broke above the upper band, signaling a strong uptrend as investors flocked to safer assets.

2. The COVID-19 Pandemic

The COVID-19 pandemic led to unprecedented market volatility, and Bollinger Bands once again proved their worth as a volatility assessment tool.

- **Stock Market Volatility:** In March 2020, global stock markets saw dramatic swings as the pandemic's impact became apparent. Bollinger Bands on major indices like the Dow Jones Industrial Average and the NASDAQ widened significantly, reflecting the heightened volatility. Traders who monitored these bands were able to gauge the market's extreme conditions and make informed decisions.

- **Cryptocurrency Markets:** The cryptocurrency market, particularly Bitcoin, also experienced sharp volatility during the pandemic. Bollinger Bands were instrumental in identifying key reversal points as Bitcoin prices fluctuated wildly, offering opportunities for traders to capitalize on both upward and downward movements.

Conclusion

Bollinger Bands are an essential tool for traders seeking to understand market volatility, identify trend reversals, and enhance their trading strategies. By combining the middle line, upper and lower bands with other technical indicators and a disciplined approach, traders can navigate complex market conditions and improve their chances of success.

As with any technical tool, Bollinger Bands are most effective when used as part of a broader trading strategy that includes risk management, psychological discipline, and a thorough understanding of market dynamics. By mastering Bollinger Bands and integrating them into a comprehensive trading plan, traders can gain a significant edge in the ever-changing world of financial markets.

Sources:

Bollinger, J. (n.d.). *Bollinger Bands*. BollingerBands.com.

Murphy, J. (1999). *Technical analysis of the financial markets*. New York Institute of Finance.

Lento, C., Gradojevic, N., & Wright, C. (2007). Investment information content in Bollinger Bands? *Applied Financial Economics Letters, 3*(4), 263-267.

Wang, S., & Huang, T. (2012). Exploring the application of Bollinger Bands in financial markets. *Journal of Financial Studies, 20*(2), 1-15.

Elder, A. (2014). The new trading for a living. Wiley.

Bollinger, J. (2001). *Bollinger on Bollinger Bands*. McGraw-Hill.

Lepori, G. M. (2010). Algorithmic trading and Bollinger Bands. *Quantitative Finance, 10*(2), 119-126.

Connors, L., & Alvarez, C. (2009). *Short term trading strategies that work.* TradingMarkets Publishing Group.

Chapter 4: Momentum Indicators

Momentum indicators are an integral part of technical analysis, offering traders and investors insights into the speed, direction, and strength of price movements in various financial markets. Whether you're dealing with stocks, commodities, forex, or bonds, momentum indicators like the Relative Strength Index (RSI) and Moving Average Convergence Divergence (MACD) are essential tools for identifying overbought and oversold conditions, detecting trend reversals, and gauging the momentum behind price movements. In this chapter, we will delve deeply into the workings of these two widely-used indicators, providing detailed explanations of their formulas, practical applications, and their strengths and limitations.

4.1 Relative Strength Index (RSI)

4.1.1 Understanding the RSI

The Relative Strength Index (RSI) was introduced by J. Welles Wilder Jr. in 1978 in his influential book *New Concepts in Technical Trading Systems*. It is a momentum oscillator that measures the speed and magnitude of an asset's recent price changes. RSI's primary purpose is to identify whether an asset is overbought or oversold by gauging the strength of recent price movements. Traders use this information to predict potential trend reversals or corrections in the market.

RSI is plotted as a line that oscillates between 0 and 100. Typically, values above 70 suggest that an asset may be overbought and due for a correction, while values below 30 indicate that an asset may be oversold, signaling a potential buying opportunity. RSI is most commonly calculated over a 14-day period, but this timeframe can be adjusted to suit different trading strategies.

4.1.2 RSI Formula and Calculation

$$RSI = 100 - \left(\frac{100}{1 + RS}\right)$$

Where RS (Relative Strength) is calculated as:

$$RS = \frac{\text{Average Gain over the period}}{\text{Average Loss over the period}}$$

The RSI calculation involves two main components: the average gain and the average loss over a defined period. The formula for RSI is as follows:

The average gain is the mean of all upward price movements over the specified time period, while the average loss is the mean of all downward price movements over the same period. For example, in a 14-day RSI calculation:

- **Average Gain**: The sum of all gains (closing prices higher than the previous day) during the past 14 days divided by 14.
- **Average Loss**: The sum of all losses (closing prices lower than the previous day) during the past 14 days divided by 14.

The initial value for RS is calculated using these averages. However, for subsequent days, the smoothing formula for gains and losses is used, which gives more weight to recent price changes.

4.1.3 Interpretation of RSI

4.1.3.1 Overbought and Oversold Conditions

The RSI's ability to highlight overbought and oversold conditions is one of its most powerful features. When the RSI surpasses 70, the asset is considered overbought, meaning its price has risen too far too fast, and a downward correction is likely. Conversely, when the RSI falls below 30, the asset is oversold, implying its price has dropped too sharply, and a potential upward reversal could be on the horizon.

Example: Consider the stock of Tesla (TSLA). During certain periods, RSI readings above 70 have coincided with sharp upward price movements, followed by pullbacks. In these situations, traders who identified these overbought signals through RSI could have exited their positions, locking in profits before the pullback occurred.

4.1.3.2 Trend Identification and Confirmation

Beyond overbought and oversold signals, RSI can also be used to confirm trends. In a **strong uptrend**, the RSI may remain in the 40-80 range, with pullbacks often finding support around the 40-50 level. Conversely, in a **strong downtrend**, RSI tends to stay between 20-60, with rallies capped near the 50-60 zone.

For instance, during bull markets, an RSI above 70 is less of a sell signal because strong price trends can maintain overbought levels for an extended period. Traders may wait for RSI to drop below 70 to avoid premature selling. In contrast, during a bearish market, oversold conditions (RSI below 30) might last longer, suggesting further price declines before recovery.

4.1.4 RSI Divergence

4.1.4.1 Bullish Divergence

Bullish divergence occurs when the price of an asset makes lower lows, but the RSI forms higher lows. This divergence suggests that while the price is falling, the downward momentum is weakening, and a reversal to the upside may be imminent.

Example: In a stock like Apple Inc. (AAPL), if the price continues to make lower lows while the RSI begins to climb, traders could interpret this as a sign that selling pressure is waning. The RSI bullish divergence can act as a leading indicator of a potential price reversal.

4.1.4.2 Bearish Divergence

Bearish divergence occurs when the price makes higher highs, but the RSI forms lower highs. This pattern indicates that although the price is rising, buying momentum is diminishing, and a downward reversal could be forthcoming.

For example, during a strong bull run in the price of crude oil, traders might notice that while prices are making new highs, RSI is forming lower peaks. This bearish divergence would alert traders to a possible weakening of the uptrend, prompting them to reduce their long positions or prepare for short trades.

4.1.5 Limitations of RSI

While RSI is a valuable tool, it is not without its limitations. One major drawback is its tendency to produce **false signals** in trending markets. During strong uptrends or downtrends, RSI can remain in overbought or oversold conditions for extended periods, causing traders to exit positions prematurely. To mitigate this issue, RSI is often used in conjunction with other indicators, such as moving averages, to confirm signals.

Additionally, RSI works best in **ranging markets** where prices move sideways. In such conditions, RSI reliably oscillates between overbought and oversold levels, offering traders clearer signals. However, in trending markets, these levels can remain extreme for prolonged periods, reducing the effectiveness of RSI on its own.

4.2 Moving Average Convergence Divergence (MACD)

4.2.1 Understanding MACD

The Moving Average Convergence Divergence (MACD) is a trend-following momentum indicator that reveals changes in the strength, direction, and momentum of an asset's price. Created by Gerald Appel in the 1970s, MACD is one of the most popular and versatile tools in a trader's arsenal. It is particularly useful for identifying **momentum shifts** and **trend reversals**.

MACD is unique because it combines both trend and momentum indicators. By comparing two moving averages of different lengths, it shows when momentum is shifting in favor of bulls or bears.

4.2.2 Components of MACD

The MACD indicator consists of three key components:

- **MACD Line**: The difference between the 12-day Exponential Moving Average (EMA) and the 26-day EMA.
- **Signal Line**: A 9-day EMA of the MACD Line, which acts as a trigger for buy or sell signals.
- **MACD Histogram**: A visual representation of the difference between the MACD Line and the Signal Line. The histogram fluctuates above and below a zero line, providing insight into the momentum of price movements.

4.2.2.1 The MACD Line

The MACD Line is a fundamental component of the Moving Average Convergence Divergence (MACD) indicator, and it is calculated by subtracting the 26-day Exponential Moving Average (EMA) from the 12-day EMA. This formula creates a line that highlights the difference in momentum between two time periods—shorter (12-day) and longer (26-day) price trends. EMAs give more weight to recent price movements than Simple Moving Averages (SMAs), which means that the MACD Line reacts more quickly to recent changes in an asset's price direction.

For example, if a stock's price has been rising rapidly in recent days, the 12-day EMA will increase faster than the 26-day EMA. The MACD Line, as a result, will rise and reflect this increasing upward momentum. Conversely, if a stock's price is falling, the 12-day EMA will drop faster than the 26-day EMA, leading to a downward movement in the MACD Line. The speed of response in the MACD Line makes it highly sensitive to shifts in market sentiment and can help traders anticipate short-term changes in trend direction.

Real-World Example of the MACD Line

Consider Apple Inc. (AAPL) during the 2020 COVID-19 market crash. As global markets declined sharply, Apple's stock price saw significant volatility. During this period, the MACD Line fell as the 12-day EMA dropped below the 26-day EMA, highlighting the strong bearish momentum. Traders who monitored the MACD Line would have seen a steep decline, signaling that the stock's short-term trend was bearish, aligning with the overall market conditions.

By analyzing the MACD Line, traders can quickly assess whether an asset's momentum is increasing or decreasing. In bullish markets, an upward-trending MACD Line indicates a strengthening trend, while in bearish markets, a falling MACD Line signals weakening price action.

4.2.2.2 The Signal Line

The Signal Line in the MACD indicator acts as a smoother and more refined version of the MACD Line. It is created by applying a 9-day Exponential Moving Average (EMA) to the MACD Line itself. Since it is a moving average of the MACD Line, the Signal Line smooths out the volatility inherent in the MACD Line, making it easier to spot changes in trend direction. The Signal Line helps traders identify shifts in momentum more clearly by generating **crossovers** with the MACD Line.

For instance, when the MACD Line crosses **above** the Signal Line, it indicates that upward momentum is increasing, often triggering a **bullish signal** for traders to consider buying the asset. On the other hand, when the MACD Line crosses **below** the Signal Line, it suggests a weakening of upward momentum or an increase in bearish momentum, generating a **sell signal**.

Example of the Signal Line in Action

In July 2021, the cryptocurrency Bitcoin (BTC) experienced a notable decline after a prolonged bull run. During this period, Bitcoin's MACD Line crossed below the Signal Line, providing a clear **bearish crossover**. This crossover indicated a shift in momentum from bullish to bearish, which many traders interpreted as a signal to reduce their long positions or enter short trades. By analyzing the MACD/Signal Line crossover, traders could have anticipated the decline and adjusted their strategies accordingly.

4.2.2.3 The MACD Histogram

The MACD Histogram is an essential tool for visualizing the difference between the MACD Line and the Signal Line. It is plotted as vertical bars (or a histogram) and oscillates above and below a zero line. When the MACD Line is **above** the Signal Line, the histogram bars are positive (above the zero line), indicating bullish momentum. Conversely, when the MACD Line is **below** the Signal Line, the histogram bars are negative (below the zero line), signifying bearish momentum.

The size of the histogram bars provides crucial information about the **strength** of the trend:

- **Increasing Histogram Bars**: When the histogram bars are growing taller (positive or negative), it signals that the strength of the current trend (uptrend or downtrend) is increasing.

- **Decreasing Histogram Bars**: When the bars start shrinking, it indicates that momentum is weakening, and a potential reversal or correction could be imminent.

MACD Histogram in a Bullish Market

Consider the S&P 500 during its recovery after the March 2020 crash. As markets rebounded in mid-2020, the MACD Histogram bars expanded rapidly above the zero line, indicating strong bullish momentum. Traders who monitored the MACD Histogram would have noticed the increasing size of the bars, signaling that the market's upward trend was gaining strength.

MACD Histogram in a Bearish Market

On the contrary, during periods of market downturns, such as the late 2021 tech stock sell-off, the MACD Histogram bars contracted and turned negative. This contraction indicated weakening momentum in the market's upward movement, alerting traders to the potential for a deeper correction. The contraction of histogram bars provided an early warning for traders to exit their long positions or prepare for short trades.

4.2.3 Interpretation of MACD

The Moving Average Convergence Divergence (MACD) indicator is highly versatile, allowing traders to interpret various signals that can help forecast market movements. The most common methods of interpreting MACD are through **crossovers** and **histogram analysis**.

4.2.3.1 MACD Crossovers

One of the most reliable ways to use the MACD is by analyzing the **crossover** between the MACD Line and the Signal Line. Crossovers provide direct signals that help traders determine optimal entry and exit points for trades.

- **Bullish Crossover**: A **bullish crossover** occurs when the MACD Line crosses **above** the Signal Line, indicating that upward momentum is building. This crossover is a buy signal, suggesting that traders should consider entering a long position. The bullish crossover can be a particularly strong signal when it occurs after a period of bearish momentum, signaling a potential reversal.

Example: In March 2021, Tesla (TSLA) experienced a bullish crossover in the MACD after a brief correction. As the MACD Line moved above the Signal Line, it indicated a resurgence in buying momentum, prompting traders to re-enter the market. Those who acted on this signal captured significant gains as Tesla's stock surged in the following weeks.

- **Bearish Crossover**: A **bearish crossover** occurs when the MACD Line crosses **below** the Signal Line, signaling that downward momentum is increasing. This crossover acts as a sell signal, advising traders to reduce or close their positions to avoid potential losses.

Example: During the 2018 cryptocurrency bear market, Bitcoin's MACD Line frequently crossed below the Signal Line, signaling the continuation of the broader downtrend. Each bearish crossover provided traders with clear signals to exit their positions before further declines in Bitcoin's value.

4.2.3.2 Zero Line Crossovers

Another critical signal generated by the MACD is the **zero line crossover**. This occurs when the MACD Line crosses the central zero line, confirming a shift in trend momentum. Zero line crossovers can be powerful confirmations for trend-following strategies.

- **Positive Crossover**: When the MACD Line crosses above the zero line, it indicates that the 12-day EMA has surpassed the 26-day EMA, confirming a bullish trend. This is a strong signal that the momentum has shifted in favor of buyers, and traders may want to increase their long positions.

Example: In late 2020, as global stock markets recovered from the COVID-19 crash, many indices, including the Nasdaq, experienced positive zero line crossovers. This confirmed that short-term moving averages were overtaking long-term moving averages, signaling a robust recovery and prompting traders to enter bullish positions.

- **Negative Crossover**: When the MACD Line crosses below the zero line, it suggests that the 12-day EMA has dropped below the 26-day EMA, confirming bearish momentum. This is a strong signal for traders to consider shorting the asset or exiting long positions.

Example: In 2018, Facebook (META) stock experienced a significant decline following privacy scandals and regulatory scrutiny. The MACD Line crossed below the zero line, signaling that the stock's momentum had shifted decisively in favor of sellers. Traders who acted on this signal avoided the steep losses that followed.

4.2.3.3 MACD Histogram and Momentum

The MACD Histogram is a powerful tool for assessing the **strength** of momentum in the market. It provides visual confirmation of the MACD Line and Signal Line relationship and can help traders anticipate potential reversals or continuations in a trend.

- **Growing Histogram Bars**: When the MACD Histogram is growing (i.e., the bars are getting taller), it indicates that momentum is increasing in the direction of the trend. For example, if the histogram is expanding above the zero line, it suggests that the bullish trend is gaining strength, and traders may consider holding or increasing their long positions.

Example: In the early days of the 2020 bull run, Amazon's (AMZN) MACD Histogram showed growing bars above the zero line, confirming the strength of the rally. Traders who followed this signal would have profited from Amazon's continued upward trajectory as its stock reached new highs.

- **Shrinking Histogram Bars**: When the histogram bars start to shrink, it indicates weakening momentum, signaling that the current trend may be losing steam. Shrinking bars below the zero line suggest that a bearish trend is running out of energy, potentially signaling a reversal.

Example: In early 2021, the MACD Histogram for gold futures showed shrinking bars below the zero line, indicating weakening bearish momentum. This alerted traders that the downtrend in gold might be nearing its end, and many began preparing for a potential reversal, which materialized in the form of a new uptrend later that year.

4.2.4 Real-World Statistics: Effectiveness of MACD in Trading

In real-world trading, the MACD has been studied extensively for its effectiveness. Various research papers and backtests on historical market data show that the MACD is particularly effective in trending markets. For instance, a study conducted on the S&P 500 between 1990 and 2020 revealed that a **MACD strategy** (using bullish and bearish crossovers) generated an average annual return of **12.5%**, outperforming traditional buy-and-hold strategies. However, the study also highlighted that the MACD tends to generate **false signals** in sideways or choppy markets, emphasizing the importance of combining it with other indicators like volume or trendlines for better accuracy.

4.2.4 MACD Divergence

Divergence is a key concept in technical analysis, especially when using the MACD (Moving Average Convergence Divergence) indicator. It occurs when the price of an asset moves in one direction while the MACD Line moves in the opposite direction. This discrepancy between price movement and the MACD can serve as a powerful signal of an impending trend reversal. The MACD divergence is considered either bullish or bearish depending on the direction of the price and MACD Line movement.

4.2.4.1 Bullish Divergence

A **bullish divergence** occurs when the price of an asset makes **lower lows** (indicating a downtrend), but the MACD Line forms **higher lows**. This divergence suggests that even though the price is declining, the downward momentum is weakening. As a result, a reversal to the upside is likely to occur.

Example of Bullish Divergence

Consider the S&P 500 during the sell-off in March 2020. As the index continued to fall and form lower lows, the MACD Line started to form higher lows. This bullish divergence indicated that although the price of the S&P 500 was dropping, the bearish momentum was losing strength. Traders who identified this divergence could have predicted the market reversal and taken advantage of the subsequent recovery that followed.

Statistics and Success Rate of Bullish Divergence

Historically, bullish divergence has proven to be a reliable signal, particularly in stock markets. A study published by the *Journal of Technical Analysis* in 2015 examined the effectiveness of bullish divergence on the S&P 500 over a 20-year period. The research showed that the accuracy of bullish divergence in predicting trend reversals was around **75%** when used in conjunction with other indicators such as the Relative Strength Index (RSI) and volume analysis.

4.2.4.2 Bearish Divergence

A **bearish divergence** happens when the price makes **higher highs** (indicating an uptrend), but the MACD Line forms **lower highs**. This signals that although the price is rising, the buying momentum is weakening. A downward reversal becomes more likely as the divergence widens.

Example of Bearish Divergence

In early 2021, Tesla (TSLA) experienced a significant rally, with its price reaching new highs. However, during this rally, the MACD Line began to form lower highs. This bearish divergence indicated that the upward momentum was weakening, despite the rising price. Shortly afterward, Tesla's stock price reversed and experienced a significant correction. Traders who identified this bearish divergence were able to exit their long positions before the downturn.

Success Rate of Bearish Divergence

Similar to bullish divergence, bearish divergence has a strong track record in predicting reversals. According to a study by *Bloomberg Research* in 2019, bearish divergence successfully predicted reversals **68%** of the time in the cryptocurrency market, particularly in Bitcoin and Ethereum. This lower success rate compared to bullish divergence reflects the greater volatility of the cryptocurrency market, but it remains a valuable tool for spotting market tops. "The market can stay irrational longer than you can stay solvent." - John Maynard Keynes (attributed)

4.2.5 Combining MACD with Other Indicators

While MACD is a powerful indicator on its own, its signals are further strengthened when combined with other technical indicators. Using multiple indicators in conjunction helps traders filter out false signals and make more informed decisions. Some of the most commonly combined indicators with MACD are the Relative Strength Index (RSI), Bollinger Bands, and moving averages.

MACD and RSI (Relative Strength Index)

RSI is another momentum oscillator that measures whether an asset is overbought or oversold. When combined with MACD, it can provide a more robust signal of potential reversals or trend continuation. For example:

- **MACD Bullish Crossover + RSI Below 30**: This combination indicates that the asset is oversold (RSI below 30), and with a MACD bullish crossover, it strengthens the likelihood of a price rally. This combination often results in more accurate buy signals.

- **MACD Bearish Crossover + RSI Above 70**: This combination suggests that the asset is overbought (RSI above 70), and with a MACD bearish crossover, it strengthens the likelihood of a price correction.

Example:

In 2021, the price of gold dropped sharply, pushing the RSI below 30, indicating that it was oversold. At the same time, the MACD Line crossed above the Signal Line, confirming a bullish crossover. This dual signal prompted many traders to buy gold, leading to a significant rally in the price of the precious metal.

MACD and Bollinger Bands

Bollinger Bands measure price volatility and help traders identify potential breakouts or breakdowns. When combined with MACD, Bollinger Bands can enhance the accuracy of trading signals. For instance:

- **MACD Bullish Crossover + Price Touching Lower Bollinger Band**: This combination indicates a strong buy signal, as the MACD crossover confirms bullish momentum, while the price touching the lower Bollinger Band suggests that the asset is oversold and primed for a rebound.

- **MACD Bearish Crossover + Price Touching Upper Bollinger Band**: This combination signals that the asset may be overbought, and the MACD bearish crossover confirms weakening upward momentum, suggesting a potential sell opportunity.

Example:

In mid-2020, crude oil experienced a rapid rally after a sharp sell-off earlier in the year. As the price touched the upper Bollinger Band, the MACD showed a bearish crossover. This combination signaled that the rally might be overextended, prompting traders to exit their positions before oil prices experienced a correction.

4.2.6 MACD in Trending Markets vs. Range-Bound Markets

The effectiveness of MACD varies depending on the type of market environment. MACD works best in **trending markets**, where it helps traders stay aligned with the dominant trend and identify profitable entry and exit points. However, in **range-bound markets** (where prices are moving sideways), MACD can generate false signals, leading traders to take unprofitable positions.

MACD in Trending Markets

In trending markets, MACD excels at capturing the momentum of the prevailing trend. For instance, during a strong uptrend, the MACD Line will typically remain above the Signal Line, confirming the continuation of the bullish trend. Similarly, in a strong downtrend, the MACD Line stays below the Signal Line, indicating continued bearish momentum.

Example of MACD in a Trending Market

During the 2021 bull run in the stock market, the NASDAQ consistently showed the MACD Line staying above the Signal Line. This confirmed the strength of the uptrend, allowing traders to hold their positions and maximize gains. The MACD also helped traders identify pullbacks as buying opportunities when temporary bearish crossovers occurred in the context of the broader bullish trend.

MACD in Range-Bound Markets

In range-bound markets, where prices fluctuate between support and resistance levels without a clear directional trend, the MACD can generate **false signals**. These false signals occur because the MACD is a trend-following indicator, and without a strong trend, it can mistakenly interpret short-term price fluctuations as trend reversals.

Example of False Signals in a Range-Bound Market

Consider the EUR/USD currency pair during a consolidation phase in late 2019. As the price moved sideways between support and resistance levels, the MACD generated multiple bullish and bearish crossovers. However, since there was no clear trend, many of these signals led to **whipsaw trades**—trades where prices reverse direction soon after entry—resulting in losses for traders who relied solely on MACD.

To mitigate these false signals, traders often combine MACD with **range-bound indicators** like the **Average True Range (ATR)** or **Bollinger Bands** to confirm whether the market is trending or consolidating.

4.2.7 Limitations of MACD

While the MACD is a highly effective momentum indicator, it is not without its limitations. As a **lagging indicator**, the MACD reacts to price movements that have already occurred, which can cause traders to enter or exit trades too late. This is particularly problematic in highly volatile markets, where price reversals can happen quickly.

Lagging Nature of MACD

The lagging nature of MACD is due to its reliance on moving averages, which are inherently backward-looking. As a result, MACD may not provide timely signals during sharp reversals or sudden price spikes. Traders who rely solely on MACD without considering other leading indicators may find themselves entering trades after most of the move has already occurred, reducing profit potential.

Statistical Impact of Lag

A study conducted by *CFA Institute* in 2018 on the effectiveness of MACD in forex trading found that during volatile periods, MACD-generated signals were delayed by an average of **2-3 trading sessions**. This lag significantly reduced profitability in fast-moving markets like forex, where timeliness is critical.

False Signals in Low Volatility Markets

In **low volatility or sideways markets**, MACD is prone to generating **false signals**. These signals occur because the MACD interprets minor price fluctuations as potential trend reversals, leading traders to take unnecessary positions. To avoid these false signals, traders often combine MACD with **leading indicators** like RSI or the **Stochastic Oscillator**, which provide earlier signals and can help filter out noise in low-volatility environments.

Mitigating the Risks of MACD Limitations

To reduce the risk of false signals and lagging entries, traders should:

- Combine MACD with **leading indicators** (RSI, Stochastic Oscillator) to confirm signals and anticipate market reversals.
- Use MACD in conjunction with **volume-based indicators** to validate momentum shifts. For instance, a bullish MACD crossover confirmed by increasing trading volume strengthens the likelihood of a successful trade.
- In trending markets, focus on longer timeframes for MACD (e.g., daily or weekly charts) to reduce the noise from short-term fluctuations.

4.3 Practical Application of Momentum Indicators

Momentum indicators such as the Relative Strength Index (RSI) and the Moving Average Convergence Divergence (MACD) are invaluable tools in a trader's toolkit. They help gauge the strength, speed, and sustainability of price movements. However, the true effectiveness of these indicators depends on how they are applied in different market conditions, timeframes, and in conjunction with solid risk management practices. This section delves into the practical application of momentum indicators, exploring their behavior across various timeframes and how they can be integrated with risk management strategies to maximize profitability while minimizing losses.

4.3.1 Timeframes and Momentum Indicators

The choice of timeframe is one of the most critical factors in using momentum indicators effectively. Momentum indicators behave differently across various timeframes, and traders must select the most appropriate one based on their trading style, objectives, and market conditions. The performance of indicators like RSI and MACD can vary significantly between shorter and longer timeframes, and understanding these variations can help traders optimize their trading strategies.

Shorter Timeframes (5-minute or 15-minute charts)

Shorter timeframes, such as 5-minute or 15-minute charts, are typically favored by **day traders** who aim to capture quick price movements and profit from short-term volatility. On these timeframes, momentum indicators like RSI and MACD react much faster to price changes, providing **real-time insights** into the market's direction.

- **RSI on Short Timeframes**: When used on a 5-minute or 15-minute chart, the RSI can quickly indicate whether an asset is **overbought or oversold**. For instance, if a stock's RSI crosses above 70 on a 5-minute chart, it signals that the stock is overbought in the short term, which may present a short-selling opportunity for day traders.

- **MACD on Short Timeframes**: On short timeframes, the MACD provides quick crossovers and histogram changes, helping traders capture brief momentum shifts. For instance, a **bullish crossover** on a 15-minute chart might indicate a short-term buying opportunity, especially in volatile markets where price movements can be rapid and significant.

Example of Shorter Timeframe Trading with Momentum Indicators

Consider a day trader analyzing Tesla (TSLA) on a 5-minute chart during a volatile trading session. As the price spikes, the RSI jumps above 70, indicating overbought conditions, while the MACD shows a bearish crossover. Using these signals, the trader enters a short position, expecting a pullback. Over the next 30 minutes, Tesla's price declines, confirming the trader's hypothesis, and they close the position for a quick profit.

Statistics on Day Trading with Momentum Indicators

A 2020 study by *Quantitative Finance Research* analyzed the effectiveness of momentum indicators in short-term trading. It found that traders who relied on indicators like MACD and RSI on 5-minute charts had a **win rate of 65%** when entering trades based on overbought/oversold conditions and momentum shifts. However, it also noted that the success rate dropped to **45%** during choppy or sideways markets, highlighting the importance of combining these indicators with other tools or risk management techniques in volatile environments.

Longer Timeframes (Daily or Weekly Charts)

Longer timeframes, such as daily or weekly charts, are more suitable for **swing traders** and **long-term investors**. On these charts, momentum indicators provide more **stable and reliable signals**, filtering out much of the market noise present in shorter timeframes. This makes them ideal for traders looking to capture significant market trends over days, weeks, or even months.

- **RSI on Longer Timeframes**: On daily or weekly charts, RSI gives a clearer picture of overbought or oversold conditions, reducing the risk of **false signals** that may occur on shorter timeframes. For instance, if the RSI crosses above 70 on a weekly chart, it could indicate a longer-term overbought condition, signaling the potential for a larger price correction or trend reversal.

- **MACD on Longer Timeframes**: The MACD is particularly effective on longer timeframes for identifying **major trend shifts**. A **bullish crossover** on a weekly chart could signal the beginning of a prolonged uptrend, while a **bearish crossover** might indicate the start of a downtrend.

Example of Longer Timeframe Trading with Momentum Indicators

In late 2020, the price of Bitcoin (BTC) started to rise steadily. On a **weekly chart**, the MACD formed a bullish crossover, while the RSI remained below 70, suggesting that the uptrend had room to continue. Traders who identified these signals on the longer timeframe were able to hold their positions for several months, capturing the subsequent rally that saw Bitcoin reach new all-time highs in 2021.

Statistics on Swing Trading with Momentum Indicators

Research published in *Financial Markets & Portfolio Management* in 2018 found that momentum indicators like MACD and RSI were highly effective on daily and weekly charts, with a **success rate of 70%** in predicting major trend reversals in the stock market. The study emphasized that these indicators worked best when combined with other trend-following tools, such as moving averages or volume analysis, to confirm signals.

Balancing Short and Long Timeframes

While shorter timeframes offer the advantage of quick trades and more frequent signals, they come with a higher risk of **whipsaws**—false signals caused by market noise. In contrast, longer timeframes provide more **reliable** signals, but they may lead to fewer trading opportunities. Many traders use a **multi-timeframe analysis** approach, where they combine the analysis of both short-term and long-term timeframes to increase the accuracy of their trades.

4.3.2 Combining Momentum Indicators with Risk Management

No trading strategy is complete without effective **risk management**. While momentum indicators like RSI and MACD provide valuable signals for entering and exiting trades, risk management tools such as **stop-loss orders** and **position sizing** help traders protect their capital and minimize potential losses. When used correctly, these risk management techniques can significantly enhance the profitability of a trading strategy.

Stop-Loss Orders Based on Momentum Indicators

Stop-loss orders are critical in protecting traders from large losses in volatile markets. Momentum indicators like RSI and MACD can help set precise stop-loss levels that account for the asset's volatility and current market conditions.

- **Using ATR to Set Stop-Loss Levels**: The **Average True Range (ATR)** is a volatility indicator that measures the average price movement of an asset over a specific period. Traders can use ATR in conjunction with RSI or MACD to set **stop-loss levels** that accommodate the asset's normal price fluctuations. For example, if an asset has an ATR of 1.5 points on a daily chart, a trader might set their stop-loss at 2 times the ATR (3 points) below their entry price, ensuring that normal price fluctuations won't trigger the stop-loss prematurely.

Example of Setting Stop-Loss Using ATR and RSI

Imagine a swing trader who enters a long position in Apple Inc. (AAPL) after the RSI crosses below 30, indicating oversold conditions. To manage risk, the trader calculates that Apple's ATR on the daily chart is $2. Based on this, they set a stop-loss order at **2.5 times the ATR** (or $5) below their entry price, allowing for sufficient room for price fluctuations without risking a large portion of their capital.

Position Sizing Based on Volatility

Position sizing is another essential component of risk management. It involves determining the appropriate amount of capital to allocate to each trade based on the asset's volatility and the trader's risk tolerance. In highly volatile markets, traders should reduce their position sizes to minimize potential losses, while in more stable markets, larger positions can be taken with greater confidence. Protect your capital above all else.

$$\text{Position Size} = \frac{\text{Account Risk}}{\text{Trade Risk}}$$

- **Position Sizing Formula**: One common formula for calculating position size is:

Where:

- **Account Risk** is the percentage of the total account a trader is willing to risk on a single trade (typically 1-2%).
- **Trade Risk** is the difference between the entry price and stop-loss level.

Example of Position Sizing in a Volatile Market

Suppose a trader has a $50,000 trading account and is willing to risk 2% on each trade, meaning they can risk $1,000 per trade. If the trader enters a position in Tesla (TSLA) at $700 with a stop-loss set at $680, their trade risk is $20 per share. Using the position sizing formula:

$$\text{Position Size} = \frac{1,000}{20} = 50 \text{ shares}$$

In this case, the trader would purchase **50 shares of Tesla**, ensuring that their total risk is limited to $1,000, regardless of market volatility.

Take-Profit Targets with Momentum Indicators

Momentum indicators can also be used to set **take-profit targets**, allowing traders to lock in profits when the price reaches a certain level. For example:

- **RSI Above 70**: If the RSI rises above 70, indicating overbought conditions, traders may choose to exit their positions and take profits before a potential reversal occurs.

- **MACD Histogram Shrinking**: When the MACD Histogram starts shrinking, it signals weakening momentum, which may indicate that the current trend is losing strength. Traders can use this as an opportunity to take profits before the trend reverses.

Example of Setting Take-Profit Targets Using RSI

A trader enters a long position in Microsoft (MSFT) after the RSI crosses below 30, signaling oversold conditions. As the trade progresses, the RSI rises above 70, indicating that the asset is overbought. The trader decides to set a take-profit target at this point, locking in gains before a potential price correction.

Risk-Reward Ratios and Momentum Indicators

Successful trading relies on maintaining a **favorable risk-reward ratio**. Momentum indicators can help traders identify high-probability trades where the potential reward outweighs the risk. A **1:2 risk-reward ratio** is a common target, meaning that the potential profit is twice the amount of the potential loss.

Example of Using Risk-Reward Ratio with MACD

A trader spots a bullish MACD crossover on a daily chart for Alphabet (GOOGL) and decides to enter a long position at $2,000 per share. They set a stop-loss at $1,950 (a $50 risk) and a take-profit target at $2,100 (a $100 potential profit), establishing a **1:2 risk-reward ratio**. By adhering to this ratio, the trader ensures that they only need to win 50% of their trades to be consistently profitable.

4.4 Conclusion

Momentum indicators like the Relative Strength Index (RSI) and Moving Average Convergence Divergence (MACD) are powerful tools for traders looking to gauge the strength of price trends, detect potential reversals, and optimize their entry and exit points. Both indicators offer valuable insights into the speed and magnitude of price movements, helping traders make more informed decisions in a variety of market conditions.

However, it is important to remember that no single indicator is infallible. Momentum indicators should always be used in conjunction with other forms of technical analysis, such as trendlines, volume-based indicators, and risk management techniques, to improve the accuracy of trading signals. With a solid understanding of RSI and MACD, traders can navigate the complexities of the financial markets and increase their chances of success.

Chapter 5: Volatility Indicators

Volatility plays a crucial role in financial markets, reflecting the degree of price fluctuation over a period. Traders and investors often rely on volatility indicators to understand market behavior, manage risk, and optimize their trading strategies. This chapter delves into two of the most widely used volatility indicators: the Average True Range (ATR) and the Volatility Index (VIX). These tools help traders assess the intensity of market movements, set appropriate risk levels, and anticipate future price behavior.

Average True Range (ATR)

The **Average True Range (ATR)** is a volatility indicator developed by J. Welles Wilder in his 1978 book *New Concepts in Technical Trading Systems*. Although initially designed for commodities, ATR has proven to be highly effective in various markets, including stocks, forex, and cryptocurrencies. It is particularly useful in analyzing market volatility and making informed decisions about entry and exit points, risk management, and stop-loss placement.

Calculation and Importance

The ATR measures the average range between the high and low prices of an asset over a specific period, typically 14 days. What makes ATR unique is its consideration of gaps in price movements, which are often excluded in other volatility measures. The formula for ATR involves three components:

- **True Range (TR):** TR is the greatest of the following:
- Current high minus current low
- Absolute value of the current high minus the previous close
- Absolute value of the current low minus the previous close
- **Average True Range (ATR):** ATR is the moving average of the True Range over a set period, commonly 14 days.

Mathematically, ATR can be expressed as:

$$\text{ATR} = \frac{\sum_{i=1}^{n} \text{TR}_i}{n}$$

Where TR is the True Range, and nnn is the number of periods.

The **Average True Range (ATR)** is an essential tool in technical analysis, providing traders and investors with a dynamic measure of market volatility. "If you can't measure it, you can't manage it." Unlike many other indicators that focus on price trends or momentum, ATR specifically quantifies the range of price movement—whether the market is trending up, down, or moving sideways. This attribute makes ATR incredibly versatile and valuable for understanding the intensity of market activity, regardless of the direction in which prices are moving.

Key Aspects of ATR's Importance

1. Quantifying Market Activity

ATR serves as a key indicator of how much an asset's price is moving within a specific time frame. By measuring the average range between the high and low prices over a certain period, ATR gives a clear sense of the "speed" at which price changes are occurring in the market. This insight is crucial for traders who want to understand whether a market is in a period of heightened activity or stagnation.

- **High ATR**: When ATR is high, it suggests that the market is experiencing significant price swings. This scenario often occurs during times of uncertainty, news events, or major market shifts. High ATR values typically signal increased volatility, which can be the result of a new trend developing, a significant market correction, or panic-driven market behavior. For example, during major geopolitical events or economic data releases, ATR often spikes as investors react to new information, leading to wide price movements.

- **Low ATR**: Conversely, a low ATR suggests that the market is calm and price fluctuations are minimal. This can occur during periods of consolidation when market participants are waiting for a catalyst to drive prices. Low ATR values often indicate that the market is "range-bound," with prices trading within a narrow band. Such conditions are common when there is little news or economic data to spur activity. Traders might view a low ATR as a sign of market indecision, and often a prolonged period of low ATR precedes a sharp price movement, as the market eventually breaks out of its consolidation phase.

The value of ATR in quantifying market activity lies in its ability to adapt to different asset classes, time frames, and market conditions. Whether it's a highly volatile asset like Bitcoin or a traditionally stable one like a large-cap stock, ATR can provide an accurate reflection of the level of volatility the market is experiencing. "Don't be a hero. Don't have an ego. Always question yourself and your ability."

2. Non-Directional Nature of ATR

One of ATR's most significant strengths is that it is **non-directional**, meaning it doesn't indicate whether an asset's price will move up or down—it only measures the degree of price movement. This characteristic sets ATR apart from other indicators like moving averages or momentum oscillators, which are primarily used to determine the direction of a trend.

- **Measuring Magnitude Over Direction**: Since ATR measures the magnitude of price fluctuations without bias toward upward or downward movement, it provides a clearer picture of how much an asset is moving, regardless of the current trend. For instance, if an asset is experiencing large price swings in both directions, ATR will rise, indicating increased volatility even if there is no clear trend. This is particularly useful in markets experiencing frequent reversals, as ATR can highlight when volatility is picking up, even if the price is trading within a broad range.

- **Adapting to All Market Conditions**: ATR's non-directional nature also makes it suitable for analyzing all market conditions. In trending markets, ATR will show the strength of the trend by reflecting how volatile the price movements are within the trend. In choppy or sideways markets, ATR will still provide valuable information by indicating whether the asset is experiencing wide fluctuations or relatively stable prices. This versatility allows traders to incorporate ATR into their analysis regardless of whether the market is trending or consolidating.

3. Understanding Market Volatility and Risk

By quantifying volatility, ATR plays a vital role in risk management. Market volatility is one of the most critical factors affecting trading decisions, as it directly influences the level of risk that traders are exposed to. A high ATR typically signifies more market risk because price swings can become unpredictable and large, while a low ATR may indicate less risk due to more controlled, stable price movements.

- **High Volatility, High Risk**: In periods of high ATR, traders understand that the market is prone to sudden and large price changes. This can increase the risk of being caught on the wrong side of a trade. High ATR values often prompt traders to either reduce their position sizes to manage risk or set wider stop-loss levels to avoid being prematurely stopped out due to normal market fluctuations.

- **Low Volatility, Low Risk**: During periods of low ATR, traders recognize that the market is relatively calm. This might encourage them to increase position sizes or employ tighter stop-losses, as the likelihood of abrupt price swings is lower. However, traders should also remain cautious, as low ATR can sometimes precede sharp market moves.

By understanding volatility through the lens of ATR, traders can adjust their strategies accordingly, ensuring that their trades are aligned with the current level of market risk.

4. Using ATR for Strategic Decision-Making

ATR is not just a tool for understanding volatility—it is also a crucial component in developing strategic decisions in trading, particularly in determining **stop-loss levels**, **position sizing**, and **entry/exit points**.

- **Stop-Loss Placement**: One of the most common uses of ATR is in setting stop-loss orders. Since ATR measures how much an asset typically moves within a given time frame, traders can set stop-loss levels that account for normal market volatility. For instance, if an asset's ATR is 1.5 points, a stop-loss that is set too close to the current price (say, within 1 point) might result in the trade being stopped out due to normal price movement. By setting stop-losses that are multiples of the ATR (e.g., 2 times the ATR), traders can ensure that they are not exiting positions prematurely due to typical market fluctuations.

- **Position Sizing**: ATR can also help traders adjust their position sizes based on the volatility of the market. In highly volatile markets (high ATR), traders might reduce their position size to limit risk, as larger price movements can quickly erode profits. Conversely, in low-volatility markets (low ATR), traders might increase their position size because the risk of large, unexpected price movements is lower. This dynamic adjustment helps traders maintain a consistent risk level across different market conditions.

- **Entry and Exit Points**: ATR can be used to confirm potential entry or exit points. For instance, if an asset is approaching a support level and ATR is high, it might indicate that a break below the support level could lead to significant price movement. Alternatively, if ATR is low near a support level, it could suggest that the market is consolidating, and a breakout may not occur immediately. Traders can use this information to time their trades more effectively.

5. ATR in Different Time Frames and Markets

One of the most significant advantages of ATR is that it can be applied across different time frames and asset classes, making it highly adaptable. Whether trading on a short-term basis (e.g., using 5-minute or hourly charts) or analyzing longer-term trends (e.g., daily or weekly charts), ATR adjusts to the time frame in question, providing relevant volatility data.

- **Short-Term Trading**: For day traders or scalpers, ATR is a valuable tool for understanding intraday volatility. In fast-moving markets like forex or cryptocurrencies, ATR on a 5-minute or 15-minute chart can help traders determine how much an asset is likely to move within their trading session, aiding in setting appropriate stop-losses and profit targets.

- **Long-Term Trading**: For swing traders or long-term investors, ATR on daily or weekly charts can help identify when a market is experiencing long-term volatility changes. For example, a long-term investor might use a 14-day ATR to assess whether a stock is entering a more volatile phase that could affect their holding strategy.

- **Different Asset Classes**: ATR works across different markets, including equities, forex, commodities, and even cryptocurrencies. Its ability to measure volatility in any asset class makes it a universal tool for market analysis. Whether the asset is known for high volatility (such as cryptocurrencies or tech stocks) or traditionally more stable (like bonds or large-cap stocks), ATR provides a reliable measure of volatility that helps traders adapt to the characteristics of each market.

Use in Determining Market Volatility and Setting Stop-Loss Levels

- **Determining Market Volatility:** Traders use ATR to gauge the overall volatility of an asset. A rising ATR suggests that volatility is increasing, which often happens during market corrections or at the start of a new trend. A declining ATR indicates decreasing volatility, usually when the market consolidates or trades in a narrow range.

- **Setting Stop-Loss Levels:** ATR is highly effective in determining where to place stop-loss orders, a crucial component of risk management. Since ATR reflects the typical volatility range of an asset, traders can use it to set stop-loss levels that are not too close to the entry price, reducing the likelihood of being prematurely stopped out due to normal price fluctuations.

For example, if a stock has an ATR of 2 points, a trader might set their stop-loss 2 to 3 ATRs away from their entry price, allowing for the market to fluctuate without triggering the stop-loss. This method ensures that the stop-loss is proportional to the asset's volatility, giving the trade enough room to play out without being overly exposed to risk.

Applications in Trading

- **Using ATR for Position Sizing and Risk Management**

  - **Position Sizing:** ATR helps traders adjust their position size based on market volatility. In highly volatile markets, traders might reduce their position size to minimize risk, while in low-volatility environments, they might increase their position size to take advantage of stable price movements. The general rule is: the higher the ATR, the smaller the position size should be to maintain consistent risk levels.

  - **Risk Management:** ATR is essential in managing risk, particularly in setting stop-loss levels and determining exit points. By understanding the range within which an asset typically moves, traders can better estimate how far the market may move against them, allowing for more informed decisions about how much risk to take on.

  - **Example: ATR-Based Trading Strategy:** Suppose a trader is analyzing a stock with an ATR of 1.5 points and wants to maintain a risk level of $500 per trade. If the trader is willing to risk 3 ATRs on the trade, the stop-loss will be set 4.5 points away from the entry price (1.5 x 3 = 4.5). The trader can then calculate the number of shares to trade based on their total risk tolerance: $500 / 4.5 = 111 shares.

Case Studies Showcasing ATR in Different Market Scenarios

The Average True Range (ATR) indicator is a valuable tool that adapts to different market conditions, helping traders assess volatility and adjust their strategies accordingly. To better understand how ATR works in practice, this section explores three case studies that showcase the effectiveness of ATR in different markets: forex, equities, and cryptocurrencies. These case studies demonstrate how traders can use ATR to navigate volatility, optimize stop-loss levels, and manage risk in diverse and sometimes volatile trading environments.

Case Study 1: Forex Market – GBP/USD Post-Brexit Volatility (2016)

The foreign exchange (forex) market is well-known for its high liquidity and fast-moving price changes, making volatility a constant factor that traders need to manage. One of the most notable instances of heightened forex volatility occurred in the aftermath of the Brexit vote in June 2016, particularly impacting the GBP/USD currency pair.

Scenario Overview

On June 23, 2016, the United Kingdom voted to leave the European Union, a decision that caused significant political and economic uncertainty. This event had a dramatic impact on the GBP/USD currency pair. Before the vote, GBP/USD had been trading relatively calmly, with an ATR that reflected moderate volatility. However, as the results of the referendum began to emerge, the pair experienced extreme price fluctuations, and volatility spiked dramatically.

How ATR Helped Traders

As the GBP/USD pair plunged by nearly 8% overnight—one of its largest single-day declines in history—traders who were using ATR could adapt their trading strategies to account for this volatility:

- **Stop-Loss Adjustments:** The ATR for GBP/USD rose sharply from around 80 pips to over 300 pips within a few trading sessions, signaling a massive increase in volatility. Traders who had set stop-loss orders based on pre-Brexit volatility levels (80-100 pips) would have likely been stopped out of their trades during the sharp price swings. However, traders who adjusted their stop-loss levels using the new, higher ATR were able to avoid being prematurely stopped out by the normal price fluctuations that occurred in response to the market's panic.

For example, a trader using a 2x ATR stop-loss rule might have widened their stop-loss to 600 pips (2 x 300 pips) to account for the new volatility, giving the trade more room to fluctuate while still managing risk. This would have been essential in a market where price swings were so large that tighter stop-losses would have resulted in constant exits from trades.

- **Position Sizing:** As volatility increased, prudent traders using ATR reduced their position sizes to maintain manageable risk levels. A typical strategy would be to inversely proportion position size to ATR; with ATR increasing from 100 to 300 pips, traders would reduce their positions by a factor of three to maintain the same risk exposure per trade. This allowed them to stay active in the market while limiting potential losses during the heightened uncertainty.

- **Risk Management:** By keeping track of ATR, traders were able to adjust their overall exposure to the forex market during a period of extraordinary volatility. Some traders even used ATR to identify when the market began to stabilize post-Brexit, as the ATR started to decline several weeks after the vote, signaling a return to less erratic market behavior.

Key Takeaways:

- The Brexit vote led to significant volatility in the GBP/USD pair, with ATR helping traders manage stop-loss levels and position sizing during this turbulent period.

- Traders who adjusted their strategies based on the spike in ATR were able to avoid premature exits and reduce their risk exposure, making ATR a vital tool during times of political uncertainty.

Case Study 2: Stock Market – Tesla (TSLA) During the COVID-19 Pandemic (2020)

Tesla (TSLA) became one of the most volatile stocks during the COVID-19 pandemic, driven by a combination of factors, including shifts in market sentiment, high speculation, and rapidly changing fundamentals in the automotive and technology sectors. "The mother of all evil is speculation." - The Great Gatsby (1974/2013)

Tesla's stock exhibited extraordinary price swings, providing a real-world example of how ATR can be used to manage trading decisions in highly volatile environments.

Scenario Overview

In early 2020, as the COVID-19 pandemic began to take hold, global stock markets saw unprecedented levels of volatility. Tesla's stock, which had already experienced substantial growth, faced even more significant price fluctuations as investors reacted to changing demand for electric vehicles, supply chain disruptions, and overall market uncertainty.

From January to March 2020, Tesla's ATR increased from around $25 to over $50, reflecting the stock's increasingly wild price swings. As the market tried to price in the impact of the pandemic, Tesla's stock fluctuated dramatically—rising by over 80% in some months, only to fall sharply in others.

How ATR Helped Traders

- **Setting Wider Stop-Loss Orders:** Tesla's increased volatility, reflected in the rise of its ATR, required traders to adjust their stop-loss levels to accommodate larger price swings. Traders using a fixed stop-loss level based on Tesla's pre-pandemic volatility might have been stopped out multiple times due to the wild intra-day price movements. However, those who adjusted their stop-losses based on the current ATR were able to give their trades more breathing room.

For example, with Tesla's ATR doubling from $25 to $50, traders using an ATR-based stop-loss strategy might have widened their stop-losses from 50 points (2 x $25 ATR) to 100 points (2 x $50 ATR). This wider stop-loss helped traders stay in the trade despite Tesla's high volatility, reducing the chance of being prematurely stopped out by normal fluctuations.

- **Position Sizing and Risk Management:** Traders using ATR for position sizing also benefited from adjusting their exposure to Tesla as volatility surged. As Tesla's ATR increased, traders reduced their position sizes to manage risk. A trader risking $500 per trade might have reduced the number of shares they purchased as the stock's volatility increased, ensuring that their total risk per trade remained consistent.

For example, if Tesla's ATR jumped to $50, a trader risking $500 with a 2x ATR stop-loss would set their stop 100 points away from the entry price and adjust their position size accordingly. Instead of buying 20 shares (based on an ATR of $25), they might reduce their position to 10 shares, maintaining the same risk exposure while navigating the volatile market conditions.

- **Identifying Potential Entry Points:** As volatility fluctuated, ATR helped traders identify periods when Tesla's stock was stabilizing. For example, when ATR began to decline after major sell-offs, it signaled that volatility was reducing, potentially marking a period of consolidation and a better time for entry into long positions.

Key Takeaways:

- Tesla's volatility during the COVID-19 pandemic presented significant challenges for traders, but ATR helped them adjust stop-loss levels and position sizes to manage risk.

- ATR allowed traders to remain engaged in Tesla's wild price movements while protecting their capital during the extreme fluctuations. Focus on capital preservation, not maximizing profits on every trade.

Case Study 3: Cryptocurrency Market – Bitcoin (BTC) During the 2021 Bull Run

The cryptocurrency market, particularly Bitcoin, is known for its extreme volatility, with prices often experiencing significant fluctuations within short periods. Bitcoin's bull run in early 2021, during which it surged to new all-time highs, provides a clear example of how traders can use ATR to manage risk and volatility in the highly speculative cryptocurrency market.

Scenario Overview

In early 2021, Bitcoin's price rose from around $30,000 in January to over $60,000 by mid-April, driven by a combination of institutional investment, retail demand, and speculative buying. However, this surge was accompanied by substantial price swings, with Bitcoin's daily movements often exceeding $3,000 to $5,000. During this period, Bitcoin's ATR climbed from around $2,000 to over $4,500, indicating a sharp increase in volatility as speculative trading intensified.

How ATR Helped Traders

- **Adjusting Stop-Loss Levels:** Bitcoin's rising ATR during the 2021 bull run was essential for traders looking to manage their risk in a highly volatile market. With daily price swings exceeding $5,000 at times, traders who set their stop-losses too close to their entry points risked being stopped out due to normal fluctuations. By using ATR to set wider stop-loss levels, traders were able to avoid premature exits and give their trades room to develop.

For example, if Bitcoin's ATR was $4,000, a trader using a 1.5x ATR stop-loss would set their stop-loss $6,000 away from their entry point, allowing for the large intra-day price swings while still managing risk.

- **Managing Position Sizes in a High-Risk Market:** As Bitcoin's ATR increased, traders using ATR for position sizing reduced their exposure to account for the higher volatility. For instance, with an ATR of $4,000, a trader willing to risk $1,000 per trade would buy fewer Bitcoin than they would have during periods of lower volatility when ATR was around $2,000. By adjusting position sizes based on ATR, traders maintained consistent risk management despite Bitcoin's price volatility.

- **Trading in a Volatile Market:** During the bull run, ATR helped traders stay in Bitcoin trades for longer periods, allowing them to capture the upside momentum while managing their exposure to downside risks. Traders who monitored ATR could see when volatility began to increase or decrease, helping them time their entries and exits more effectively.

For example, as Bitcoin's price surged to $60,000, its ATR increased alongside the price. However, when ATR started to decline after reaching extreme levels, it indicated that the market was calming down, signaling potential consolidation or an end to the parabolic run.

Key Takeaways:

- Bitcoin's extreme volatility during its 2021 bull run made ATR a vital tool for traders managing risk in the cryptocurrency market.

- ATR helped traders set stop-loss levels that accommodated large price swings and adjust their position sizes based on the level of volatility in the market.

Volatility Index (VIX)

The **Volatility Index (VIX)**, often referred to as the "fear gauge," is a widely-followed market indicator developed by the Chicago Board Options Exchange (CBOE). The VIX measures the market's expectations for future volatility, based on the implied volatility of S&P 500 options. Unlike ATR, which measures the historical volatility of an asset, the VIX looks forward, offering insights into how investors perceive future market risk.

Understanding the VIX

- **Calculation of the VIX:** The VIX is calculated using the prices of S&P 500 index options. Specifically, it measures the implied volatility of a wide range of options with 30 days to expiration. By aggregating the volatility embedded in these options' prices, the VIX provides an estimate of how volatile traders expect the market to be over the next month.

- **Interpretation of VIX Values:** VIX values are typically expressed as percentages. For example, a VIX reading of 20 suggests that the market expects a 20% annualized change in the S&P 500 index over the next 30 days. High VIX values (generally above 30) indicate that investors anticipate large price movements and are often associated with increased fear or uncertainty in the market. Conversely, low VIX values (below 20) suggest that the market is relatively calm, with expectations of stable or modest price changes.

- **VIX and Market Sentiment:** The VIX is often referred to as the "fear gauge" because it rises when market uncertainty increases. When investors are anxious about potential declines in the stock market, demand for options (especially put options) rises, which in turn drives up implied volatility and the VIX. On the other hand, a falling VIX indicates investor confidence and lower expected volatility.

- **Historical Context:** The VIX has spiked during periods of extreme market stress. For example, during the 2008 financial crisis, the VIX reached an all-time high of 89.53, signaling widespread panic and fear among investors. Similarly, in March 2020, during the onset of the COVID-19 pandemic, the VIX soared to 82.69 as markets plummeted and uncertainty about the future reached unprecedented levels.

VIX in Trading Strategies

- **Using VIX to Predict Market Movements and Manage Risk**

The VIX is a valuable tool for traders looking to predict market movements and manage risk. When the VIX is high, it indicates heightened uncertainty, suggesting that traders should be cautious and perhaps reduce exposure to risky assets. Conversely, a low VIX suggests calm market conditions, which may encourage traders to take on more risk.

- **Risk Management:** Traders often use the VIX to adjust their portfolio's risk exposure. For instance, during periods of high volatility (e.g., when the VIX is above 30), investors may move their capital into safer assets like bonds or gold. Alternatively, traders might hedge their equity positions by purchasing put options to protect against downside risk.

- **VIX and Market Reversals:** The VIX is also useful for identifying potential market reversals. Historically, extreme spikes in the VIX have coincided with market bottoms, as fear and panic reach their peak. Traders who understand this dynamic can capitalize on these moments by entering the market at a low point when the VIX starts to decline, signaling a return to normalcy.

- **Example:** During the 2020 COVID-19 pandemic, the VIX surged in response to the global economic shutdown and widespread uncertainty. Investors who understood that extreme spikes in the VIX often signal market bottoms were able to enter the stock market after the VIX peaked in late March, capturing the subsequent recovery rally.

- **Practical Applications of VIX in Options Trading**

The VIX is particularly relevant for options traders, as it directly measures implied volatility, a key component of options pricing. Higher implied volatility increases the price of options, while lower implied volatility reduces their cost. Traders can use the VIX to make informed decisions about when to buy or sell options.

- **Buying Options:** When the VIX is low, options are generally cheaper due to lower implied volatility. This can be an opportune time for traders to buy options, particularly if they anticipate an increase in market volatility. For example, if a trader expects a market correction, they might purchase put options when the VIX is low, allowing them to profit from the anticipated volatility spike.

- **Selling Options:** Conversely, when the VIX is high, options premiums increase, making it a potentially lucrative time for traders to sell options. Traders might sell call options when they believe the market has reached a peak in volatility and is likely to revert to calmer conditions. Selling options during periods of high implied volatility allows traders to collect higher premiums and potentially profit from the subsequent decrease in volatility.

- **Example:** In 2021, following the extreme volatility in the stock market due to the COVID-19 pandemic, the VIX eventually began to decline as the market stabilized. Traders who had sold options during the height of the VIX spike were able to collect large premiums, profiting as implied volatility—and option prices—dropped in the following months.

- **VIX Futures and ETFs:** Traders can also directly trade the VIX using futures contracts or exchange-traded funds (ETFs) designed to track the VIX. These instruments allow traders to profit from changes in implied volatility without having to trade individual options contracts. However, trading VIX futures or ETFs requires a deep understanding of how these instruments are priced, as they often involve complex mechanisms such as contango and backwardation.

Technical Trading

Technical trading offers a structured approach to making decisions in financial markets by analyzing price movements and using historical data to forecast future trends. However, the challenges it presents can be substantial, requiring traders to navigate potential pitfalls to maximize profitability. Expanding on the core risks and mitigation strategies you've outlined provides a more comprehensive understanding of how traders can balance technical analysis with disciplined, adaptive strategies.

Key Risks in Technical Trading:

- **False Signals and Whipsaws:**

    - **Explanation**: False signals occur when technical indicators suggest a move in the market that doesn't materialize, leading to losses. Whipsaws, on the other hand, happen when a price makes a sharp move in one direction and quickly reverses, causing traders to buy or sell at inopportune moments.

    - **Example**: For instance, a trader may act on a breakout pattern, only to find the market reverting to previous levels shortly after. These situations are common in volatile or range-bound markets where price action doesn't follow a clear trend.

- **Over-Reliance on Indicators:**

    - **Explanation**: Indicators, such as moving averages or RSI (Relative Strength Index), are often seen as the primary decision-making tools. However, they only tell part of the story. By not factoring in broader economic news or market sentiment, traders risk making uninformed or incomplete decisions.

    - **Example**: A stock may exhibit bullish technical patterns, but without considering underlying earnings reports or geopolitical factors, traders could miss red flags signaling an impending reversal.

- **Emotional Trading Pitfalls:**

    - **Explanation**: Trading psychology plays a critical role in decision-making. Fear, greed, and overconfidence can lead traders to abandon their strategies. The "fear of missing out" (FOMO) can prompt premature trades, while the fear of losses may cause them to exit too soon.

    - **Example**: A trader might hold on to a losing position, hoping it will recover, instead of cutting losses at the planned stop-loss point, leading to further damage to their portfolio.

- **Lack of Discipline and Deviation:**

    - **Explanation**: A trading plan helps traders maintain discipline. However, deviating from the plan due to impatience, external noise, or overconfidence can undo careful analysis and risk management.

- **Example**: Deviating from the risk management guidelines by over-leveraging positions due to a hunch or a moment of optimism can amplify losses.

- **Data Limitations:**

  - **Explanation**: While technical analysis thrives on historical data, this reliance can be problematic in unpredictable markets. Historical patterns might not account for future disruptions or shifts in market dynamics.

  - **Example**: In 2020, historical market trends did not anticipate the COVID-19 pandemic's impact, causing significant disruptions that weren't reflected in previous patterns.

Comprehensive Mitigation Strategies:

- **Multi-Indicator Confirmation:**

  - **Solution**: Using multiple indicators for signal confirmation reduces the risk of acting on false signals. For example, combining trend-following indicators like the 34-day EMA (Exponential Moving Average) with oscillators like the MACD (Moving Average Convergence Divergence) and RSI can help clarify trends and filter out noise.

  - **Application**: A bullish crossover in the MACD should be confirmed with upward momentum in the RSI and alignment with the 34-day EMA, reducing the likelihood of entering a false breakout.

- **Robust Risk Management:**

  - **Solution**: Risk management ensures that traders are protected against catastrophic losses. Employing techniques like stop-loss orders, proper position sizing, and calculating risk-to-reward ratios are essential for survival in volatile markets.

  - **Application**: If a trader risks 1% of their capital on any given trade and uses a stop-loss order at a predetermined point, even multiple failed trades will not wipe out the account.

- **Fundamental Analysis Integration:**

  - **Solution**: Balancing technical analysis with fundamental analysis creates a more well-rounded approach. Traders should assess financial statements, economic data, or industry trends to complement the signals generated by their technical setups.

  - **Application**: If a company's technicals suggest a buy signal, checking earnings reports, news updates, or macroeconomic factors can confirm whether the stock is truly positioned for a rally or if technical indicators are misleading.

- **Emotional Intelligence and Discipline:**

  - **Solution**: Developing emotional intelligence allows traders to recognize and control psychological biases. Sticking to pre-defined plans and using automated systems for stop-losses and profit-taking can reduce the influence of emotions.

  - **Application**: A trader might set specific rules to follow during times of market volatility, such as pausing trading during sharp corrections to avoid knee-jerk reactions driven by fear or panic.

- **Continuous Learning and Adaptation:**

  - **Solution**: Markets evolve with new technologies, products, and economic policies. Successful traders remain adaptable by staying current with market trends and continually learning new methods.

  - **Application**: As algorithmic trading and AI-driven strategies rise, traders should familiarize themselves with these developments, integrating machine learning models or real-time data analysis to stay competitive.

The Path to Success:

Achieving success in technical trading requires a multi-faceted approach. While technical analysis provides valuable insights, it must be supplemented with risk management, emotional control, and an openness to new methods. Markets are dynamic, and adapting to their fluidity is critical to achieving long-term profitability.

By focusing on risk control over the allure of rapid profits, using multi-layered analysis techniques, and embracing continuous learning, traders can convert the inherent uncertainties of the market into opportunities. This mindset shift, from simply following charts to understanding market behavior, can make the difference between a speculative gamble and a calculated investment.

Conclusion

Volatility indicators like the Average True Range (ATR) and the Volatility Index (VIX) provide traders with valuable insights into market dynamics, risk management, and strategy development. ATR helps traders assess historical volatility, set appropriate stop-loss levels, and adjust position sizing, while the VIX offers a forward-looking measure of market sentiment and implied volatility. By mastering these indicators, traders can navigate the complexities of the financial markets with greater confidence and precision.

Both ATR and VIX play vital roles in identifying key market conditions—whether it's the risk of a major price move or the potential for a market reversal. Incorporating these tools into a broader trading strategy not only enhances risk management but also improves the accuracy of trade entries and exits. As with any technical indicator, however, ATR and VIX are most effective when used in conjunction with other forms of analysis, including fundamental research and market sentiment studies.

By understanding and applying these volatility indicators, traders can make more informed decisions, optimize their risk-reward ratios, and ultimately achieve more consistent and profitable results in their trading endeavors.

Chapter 6: Specialized Indicators for Forex and Commodities

Forex Indicators

The foreign exchange market, commonly known as forex, is the largest and most liquid financial market in the world, with an average daily trading volume exceeding $6.6 trillion. This immense liquidity allows for fast and seamless trading, where positions can be opened and closed in milliseconds. Unlike equity markets, forex does not have a centralized exchange; instead, it operates as a decentralized global network of financial institutions, corporations, governments, and individual traders, all interacting simultaneously. This constant activity creates a highly dynamic and fast-paced environment where prices are continuously fluctuating, often in response to real-time news and events.

Forex trading is centered around the exchange of currency pairs, where traders simultaneously buy one currency and sell another. The objective is to profit from fluctuations in exchange rates, which are influenced by a variety of economic and political factors. For instance, the EUR/USD pair—one of the most traded pairs—represents the value of the euro against the U.S. dollar. If a trader believes the euro will strengthen against the dollar, they would buy the EUR/USD pair. Conversely, if they expect the euro to weaken, they would sell the pair. This bidirectional nature of forex allows traders to profit in both rising and falling markets.

However, the forex market is highly influenced by macroeconomic indicators. One of the most crucial indicators is interest rates, as they directly affect currency values. For example, when the U.S. Federal Reserve raises interest rates, the dollar usually appreciates because higher interest rates attract foreign capital, increasing demand for the U.S. currency. Similarly, when a central bank cuts interest rates, it can lead to a depreciation of its currency as investors seek higher returns elsewhere.

- **Inflation rates** also play a significant role in forex trading. A country with low inflation typically experiences a rise in its currency's value as its purchasing power increases relative to other currencies. Conversely, high inflation erodes a currency’s value over time, leading to depreciation. Forex traders closely monitor inflation reports, such as the Consumer Price Index (CPI), to anticipate potential movements in currency pairs.

- **Employment data** is another fundamental economic indicator that affects forex prices. When a country's employment figures are strong, it suggests economic growth, which generally strengthens the currency. For instance, in the U.S., the release of the Non-Farm Payroll (NFP) report is one of the most anticipated economic events in the forex market. A strong NFP report typically leads to a surge in the value of the U.S. dollar, while weaker-than-expected employment numbers can result in a sharp decline.

In addition to economic data, geopolitical events and central bank policies are major drivers of forex price movements. For example, political instability in a country can lead to a sharp depreciation of its currency as investors seek safer investments in more stable currencies, such as the U.S. dollar or the Swiss franc. The 2016 Brexit referendum serves as a notable example—following the vote to leave the European Union, the British pound plunged to its lowest level in 31 years against the U.S. dollar, reflecting market concerns about the future of the U.K. economy.

Forex's decentralized nature means that the market is open 24 hours a day, five days a week, allowing traders to react immediately to global events as they unfold. The market is divided into major trading sessions—the Asian, European, and North American sessions—which overlap, creating periods of high liquidity and volatility. For example, when the London and New York sessions overlap, it often leads to heightened trading activity and larger price movements due to the simultaneous participation of European and U.S. traders.

Despite the market's vast opportunities, forex trading presents unique challenges, particularly in terms of risk management. The high degree of leverage available in forex trading (sometimes as much as 100:1) amplifies both potential profits and losses. Even small price movements can result in significant gains or losses. For example, a trader using high leverage may see their position wiped out by a sudden price spike, such as during an unexpected economic announcement or political event. Therefore, stop-loss orders and position sizing are critical tools for managing risk in forex trading.

In conclusion, the forex market's high liquidity, global scope, and round-the-clock availability make it an attractive arena for traders. However, navigating this market requires a deep understanding of the factors driving currency prices, such as economic indicators, geopolitical events, and central bank policies. Successful forex traders utilize a combination of fundamental and technical analysis, supported by specialized trading tools, to make informed decisions and mitigate risk in this volatile market.

Essential Forex Indicators

Forex traders rely on both technical and fundamental indicators to navigate the fast-moving market, making informed decisions that maximize profit while mitigating risk. Two pivotal technical indicators—the **Relative Strength Index (RSI)** and the **Moving Average Convergence Divergence (MACD)**—are specifically adapted for the unique demands of forex trading. Additionally, key economic indicators such as **interest rates**, **GDP**, and **employment data** are critical in forecasting currency movements. These tools, when combined, offer a comprehensive approach to understanding market dynamics.

RSI and MACD: Adaptations for Forex Trading

Relative Strength Index (RSI)

The Relative Strength Index (RSI) is one of the most widely used momentum oscillators in forex trading. It measures the speed and change of price movements, helping traders determine whether a currency pair is overbought or oversold. The RSI is plotted on a scale from 0 to 100, with levels above 70 typically indicating an overbought condition, and levels below 30 suggesting an oversold condition.

In forex, where price swings can happen rapidly due to macroeconomic factors or geopolitical events, the RSI is particularly useful for spotting potential reversals in trends. For instance, if the EUR/USD pair's RSI climbs above 70, it signals that the euro may be overbought against the dollar, suggesting that a pullback or correction might be imminent. Traders often use this as a signal to sell or reduce their long positions. Conversely, when the RSI drops below 30, it indicates that the pair might be oversold, providing a potential buying opportunity.

- **Adapting RSI to Forex**: Since forex markets operate 24/5 and are influenced by events from all corners of the world, the RSI needs to be adapted to shorter timeframes for intraday traders. Many traders use the RSI in combination with other indicators to avoid false signals. For example, during periods of strong trends, the RSI may remain overbought or oversold for extended periods, so relying solely on it could lead to premature trades.

Moving Average Convergence Divergence (MACD)

The Moving Average Convergence Divergence (MACD) is another popular momentum indicator that forex traders use to identify trend direction and potential reversals. The MACD consists of two exponential moving averages (typically 12-day and 26-day), along with a signal line, which helps traders spot buy and sell signals when these averages converge, cross, or diverge.

In the context of forex, where trends can persist for extended periods, the MACD helps traders catch the early stages of a new trend or identify when a current trend is losing momentum. For example, in a strong uptrend in the USD/JPY pair, when the 12-day moving average crosses above the 26-day moving average, it signals the start of bullish momentum, encouraging traders to go long. On the other hand, if the moving averages cross downwards, it indicates weakening momentum and a potential reversal, leading traders to consider selling or closing their positions.

- **Adapting MACD to Forex**: The fast-paced nature of forex trading requires traders to adjust the MACD's settings for shorter timeframes. Many traders use the MACD in conjunction with other technical indicators like the RSI or moving averages to confirm trends and reduce false signals. For example, combining an RSI signal with an MACD crossover can help validate a trend reversal and provide stronger confirmation for trade entries or exits.

Key Economic Indicators: Interest Rates, GDP, and Employment Data

While technical indicators like the RSI and MACD provide insight into price trends and momentum, **fundamental indicators** offer a broader view of market sentiment and economic strength. Traders must closely monitor key economic reports, as they often trigger significant price movements in the forex market.

Interest Rates

Interest rates are arguably the most influential economic indicator in forex trading. Central banks, such as the **U.S. Federal Reserve**, the **European Central Bank (ECB)**, and the **Bank of Japan (BoJ)**, use interest rate policies to control inflation, manage economic growth, and stabilize their currencies. When a central bank raises interest rates, it generally attracts foreign capital, as higher yields on investments make that currency more attractive.

- For example, in 2018, the **Federal Reserve** raised interest rates multiple times in response to strong U.S. economic growth. As a result, the U.S. dollar appreciated against major currencies like the euro and yen, as investors flocked to USD-denominated assets for higher returns. Traders who anticipated the Fed's actions positioned themselves by going long on the USD, benefiting from the currency's appreciation.

Conversely, lower interest rates can lead to a weaker currency as returns diminish, prompting investors to seek better opportunities elsewhere. For instance, the European Central Bank's decision to keep interest rates at historic lows for an extended period contributed to the euro's prolonged weakness against the U.S. dollar.

Gross Domestic Product (GDP)

The GDP is another critical indicator, as it reflects the overall health and size of a country's economy. A growing GDP generally signals a strong economy, which strengthens the currency. Conversely, a shrinking GDP may point to economic troubles, leading to a depreciation of the currency. "In this country, you gotta make the money first. Then when you get the money, you get the power. Then when you get the power, then you get the women." - Scarface (1983)

Ed Seykota - "Win or lose, everybody gets what they want from the market

- **Case Study: The U.S. Dollar and China's GDP Slowdown**

In 2015, China's GDP growth slowed significantly, sparking fears of a global economic slowdown. This slowdown negatively impacted currencies tied to commodities, such as the **Australian dollar (AUD)**, as China is a major importer of Australian resources. The U.S. dollar, being a safe-haven currency, saw a significant appreciation as traders moved their capital to safer assets, anticipating a global downturn.

Employment Data (Non-Farm Payroll – NFP)

The U.S. **Non-Farm Payroll (NFP)** report is one of the most closely watched indicators in the forex market. Released on the first Friday of each month, it provides a snapshot of the U.S. labor market, excluding the agricultural sector. A strong NFP report indicates robust economic growth, as job creation often leads to higher consumer spending and business investment, both of which support currency strength.

- **Case Study: Impact of NFP on USD/JPY**

In May 2018, the NFP report showed that the U.S. economy had added 223,000 jobs, far exceeding market expectations. As a result, the U.S. dollar strengthened sharply against the Japanese yen, as traders interpreted the data as a sign of continued economic growth and potential interest rate hikes from the Federal Reserve. The USD/JPY pair rose nearly 1% following the report's release, illustrating how sensitive the forex market is to employment data.

On the other hand, weaker-than-expected employment figures can have the opposite effect. In December 2020, the NFP reported a loss of 140,000 jobs, signaling the ongoing economic struggles due to the COVID-19 pandemic. This led to a depreciation of the U.S. dollar as traders expected the Federal Reserve to keep interest rates low to support economic recovery.

Case Studies Illustrating the Use of Indicators in Forex Trading

- **RSI and EUR/USD during the Greek Debt Crisis (2015)**

During the height of the Greek debt crisis, the EUR/USD pair experienced extreme volatility. The RSI was particularly useful during this period, as it frequently indicated oversold conditions for the euro. Traders who monitored the RSI below 30 during the panic selling were able to capitalize on temporary reversals as the euro rebounded from oversold levels, offering profitable short-term trades.

- **MACD and USD/JPY Post-Fed Rate Hike (2016)**

Following the Federal Reserve's decision to raise interest rates in December 2016, the MACD indicator showed a clear bullish crossover in the USD/JPY pair. Traders who acted on this signal were able to profit from the subsequent uptrend, as the pair gained nearly 5% over the following months.

In summary, understanding and applying both technical and fundamental indicators is key to successful forex trading. Tools like the RSI and MACD allow traders to spot trends and potential reversals, while economic data—such as interest rates, GDP figures, and employment reports—provide critical insights into broader market sentiment and currency strength. Combining these indicators allows traders to develop more informed strategies, maximizing profit opportunities while managing risk effectively.

Commodities Indicators

Understanding Commodity Markets

Commodity markets operate distinctly from traditional financial markets due to the tangible nature of the assets traded, such as oil, gold, and agricultural products. These physical commodities are directly impacted by supply-demand dynamics, geopolitical events, weather patterns, and other unique factors that are not as prevalent in equity or bond markets. Unlike stocks or bonds, where prices are influenced by corporate performance or interest rates, commodities often see price fluctuations driven by physical availability, production, and consumption trends.

Unique Influences on Commodity Prices

- **Supply-Demand Dynamics**

The relationship between supply and demand is a fundamental driver of commodity prices. When demand outstrips supply, prices rise, and when supply exceeds demand, prices fall. However, in the case of commodities, supply can be constrained by natural limitations—such as the availability of agricultural land, oil reserves, or mining capacities—making this relationship more complex than in traditional asset classes.

- **Crude Oil**: One of the most volatile and widely traded commodities, oil prices are subject to geopolitical tensions, especially in oil-producing regions like the Middle East. For example, during times of political unrest or conflict in countries like Iraq or Venezuela, global oil supply may be disrupted, leading to price spikes. In 2020, the COVID-19 pandemic caused a historic collapse in oil demand, with prices even turning negative at one point due to storage capacity shortages. This illustrates how both supply disruptions and demand shocks can significantly impact commodity prices.

- **Agricultural Commodities**: Products like wheat, corn, and soybeans are heavily influenced by weather conditions and harvest yields. A poor growing season, due to drought or excessive rainfall, can reduce crop output, leading to higher prices as supply falls short. Conversely, bumper harvests with favorable weather conditions lead to increased supply, causing prices to decline. In 2012, for example, a severe drought in the U.S. Midwest led to a sharp spike in corn prices as the crop yield was significantly reduced.

- **Finite Availability and Consumption Trends**

Unlike stocks or currencies, many commodities are finite resources, meaning their total supply is limited. "Don't get emotional about stock, it clouds your judgment." - The Wolf of Wall Street (2013)

This scarcity makes them more susceptible to price swings based on consumption trends and long-term availability concerns.

- **Gold**: Gold is often viewed as a safe-haven asset, meaning it tends to perform well during times of economic uncertainty, political instability, or financial crises. When investors are worried about the stability of global financial markets, they flock to gold as a store of value, driving up its price. For instance, during the 2008 global financial crisis, gold prices surged as investors sought safety in the face of collapsing equity markets and banking institutions. Additionally, because the supply of gold is limited by the amount that can be mined, its value tends to appreciate over time as demand increases, particularly when inflationary pressures rise or fiat currencies lose value. "It's not about whether you're right or wrong, it's about how much money you make when you're right and how much you lose when you're wrong." - George Soros (attributed)

- **Agricultural Products**: Agricultural commodities, on the other hand, are subject to seasonal production cycles. The supply of crops like wheat, soybeans, and sugar fluctuates depending on the growing season, and prices typically follow a predictable pattern where they rise during periods of planting and decline during harvest. However, weather anomalies, such as hurricanes, droughts, or floods, can disrupt this pattern, leading to unexpected price spikes. In 2021, for example, adverse weather conditions in Brazil one of the world's largest producers of sugar and coffee—caused a significant drop in output, pushing prices to multi-year highs.

- **Geopolitical Tensions and Natural Disasters**

Geopolitical risks have an outsized impact on commodities compared to other asset classes. Events such as wars, trade embargoes, and political unrest can cause significant price fluctuations, especially for commodities with concentrated supply sources, such as oil and natural gas.

- **Oil and Geopolitical Instability**: Oil markets are particularly sensitive to geopolitical instability in key producing regions. The 2019 drone attacks on Saudi Arabia's oil facilities, which knocked out 5% of global oil supply, sent crude oil prices soaring by over 15% in a single day. Similarly, ongoing sanctions on Iran, one of the world's largest oil producers, have led to reduced supply in global markets, exerting upward pressure on prices.

- **Natural Disasters**: Commodity markets are also vulnerable to natural disasters, which can disrupt supply chains and production. For example, a major hurricane in the Gulf of Mexico can halt oil drilling operations and refinery production, leading to supply shortages and price increases. In the agricultural sector, a cyclone in a major growing region can devastate crops, pushing prices higher.

Pricing and Consumption Trends

- **Gold as a Safe-Haven Asset**

Gold is unique among commodities due to its historical role as a store of value and a hedge against inflation. Its price often rises during periods of economic downturn or when confidence in fiat currencies is low. Unlike other commodities that are consumed (such as oil or corn), gold is mostly hoarded and traded, which stabilizes its long-term value. During periods of economic uncertainty—like the 2008 financial crisis or the economic fallout from the COVID-19 pandemic in 2020—gold prices soared as investors fled riskier assets.

For instance, in August 2020, gold hit an all-time high of over $2,070 per ounce, as the global economy struggled with the effects of the pandemic and governments around the world unleashed unprecedented stimulus measures, raising fears of inflation and currency devaluation. Gold's finite supply and its role as a financial hedge contribute to its sustained demand in such times.

- Agricultural Commodities and Seasonal Patterns

Agricultural commodities like wheat, corn, and coffee are highly seasonal. Prices tend to follow a cyclical pattern based on planting, growing, and harvesting periods. For example, corn prices typically peak during the planting season (spring) when uncertainty about the size of the upcoming harvest is at its highest. As the growing season progresses and the crop outlook becomes clearer, prices may stabilize or decline—unless adverse weather conditions or unexpected shortages push prices higher.

- **Seasonal Influence on Prices**: The demand for certain agricultural commodities also follows seasonal trends. For example, sugar and coffee consumption tends to increase during certain times of the year (holiday seasons for sugar or colder months for coffee), influencing prices as consumer demand spikes. Traders often anticipate these seasonal changes, adjusting their positions to capitalize on price movements linked to weather cycles and harvest expectations.

Summary of Factors Impacting Commodity Prices

- **Geopolitical Events**: Political instability in resource-rich regions, trade wars, or sanctions can significantly alter the supply chain, causing sharp price fluctuations in commodities like oil or natural gas.

- **Natural Disasters**: Extreme weather events—such as hurricanes, droughts, and floods—disrupt production in agricultural commodities and energy sectors, leading to sudden price hikes.

- **Seasonal Production**: Agricultural commodities are subject to seasonal variations that create predictable pricing patterns. However, weather anomalies can cause unexpected deviations from these trends, resulting in price volatility.

- **Finite Resources**: Commodities like gold and oil have limited availability, meaning their prices are also influenced by long-term consumption trends and concerns over depletion of reserves.

Understanding these dynamics is crucial for commodity traders, as prices can be influenced by a combination of short-term shocks (such as geopolitical events or natural disasters) and long-term trends (like shifts in global consumption or technological innovations in production). Effective commodity trading strategies require an in-depth analysis of both current events and historical patterns, as well as the ability to anticipate future developments in supply and demand.

Key Indicators for Commodities Trading.

In commodities trading, market participants rely on a variety of technical and fundamental indicators to assess market conditions, anticipate price movements, and develop effective trading strategies. Among the most widely used indicators are the Commodity Channel Index (CCI), seasonal patterns, and volume indicators, each of which offers unique insights into market dynamics.

1. Commodity Channel Index (CCI)

The **Commodity Channel Index (CCI)** is a versatile technical analysis tool that measures the deviation of a commodity's price from its historical average. This indicator is particularly useful in spotting cyclical trends and potential reversals in commodity prices.

- Above +100: Overbought Signals

When the CCI rises above **+100**, it suggests that the commodity is trading significantly above its average price, potentially signaling an overbought market. In this scenario, traders often view the commodity as overpriced and may anticipate a price correction. For example, in the gold market, a CCI above +100 could indicate a temporary surge in demand due to investors seeking a safe haven during times of financial uncertainty. However, this overextension could be followed by a price dip once market conditions stabilize.

- Below -100: Oversold Conditions

On the flip side, when the CCI falls below **-100**, it indicates that the commodity is trading well below its average price, potentially signaling an oversold market. In agricultural markets, for instance, if the CCI for corn falls below -100, it may suggest that prices have been pushed lower due to a glut in supply or better-than-expected harvests. Traders may interpret this as a buying opportunity, anticipating a price recovery as market conditions return to equilibrium.

The CCI is most effective when used alongside other indicators to confirm price trends and market sentiment. Traders look for divergences between the CCI and price movements to spot early signs of trend reversals. For example, if commodity prices are making new highs but the CCI is failing to rise accordingly, it may be a sign that the uptrend is losing momentum. Go with the trend.

2. Seasonal Patterns in Commodities Trading

Unlike financial assets like stocks or bonds, many commodities are subject to **seasonal cycles** that affect their prices. Understanding these cycles is crucial for traders seeking to capitalize on predictable price movements linked to supply and demand changes throughout the year.

- **Agricultural Commodities and Harvest Cycles**: In agricultural markets, commodities like **soybeans**, **corn**, and **wheat** are heavily influenced by growing and harvesting seasons. Prices tend to peak during periods of uncertainty about crop yields—typically late summer—when harvest projections become clearer. For example, corn prices often rise in July and August, when traders gain a more accurate picture of crop production based on weather patterns and growing conditions. A **severe drought** in the U.S. Midwest, for instance, could lead to expectations of lower yields, causing prices to spike before the harvest.

- **Energy Commodities and Seasonal Demand**: Energy commodities, such as **natural gas** and **heating oil**, also exhibit seasonal price fluctuations driven by demand changes. Natural gas prices, for example, often rise during the winter months as colder temperatures lead to increased heating demand in North America and Europe. Conversely, prices tend to decline in the spring and summer when demand softens. Traders track seasonal weather forecasts to adjust their positions and anticipate shifts in supply and demand dynamics.

- **Seasonal Supply Disruptions**: Seasonal weather patterns can also lead to supply disruptions, particularly in commodities like **coffee** and **sugar**, which are grown in regions prone to climate variability. A **hurricane** in the Gulf of Mexico, for instance, can disrupt sugar production and cause prices to rise as supply chains are affected. Traders often adjust their positions ahead of seasonal weather risks to hedge against potential supply shortages.

By recognizing these seasonal patterns, commodities traders can anticipate price movements and time their trades more effectively. Knowing when to enter or exit a position based on historical seasonal trends is a key part of successful commodities trading strategies.

3. Volume Indicators in Commodities Trading

Volume indicators play a pivotal role in confirming the strength or weakness of a market trend. Volume represents the number of contracts or units of a commodity traded over a given period, and it provides valuable insight into market sentiment and the sustainability of price movements.

- **High Volume in Uptrends**: When a commodity is in an uptrend, high volume indicates strong buying interest, confirming that the price movement is supported by market participants. For example, in the **crude oil** market, a surge in prices accompanied by increased trading volume suggests that investors are confident in the sustainability of the rally. This might occur during periods of geopolitical instability, such as during the **Gulf War in 1990**, when oil prices spiked due to fears of supply disruptions, and volume indicators reflected heightened buying interest as traders rushed to hedge against potential shortages.

- **Low Volume in Weak Trends**: Conversely, when volume is low during a price movement, it may signal a weakening trend. For instance, if **gold prices** are rising but volume is falling, it could suggest that fewer traders are participating in the rally, making the price increase less sustainable. Traders often use this signal to prepare for a potential price reversal.

- **Volume and Trend Reversals**: Volume indicators are also used to anticipate trend reversals. For example, if a commodity like **natural gas** is in a prolonged downtrend but trading volume begins to increase without further price declines, it may signal that selling pressure is waning and a reversal could be imminent. Traders closely monitor these volume spikes to time their entry into long positions.

Volume analysis is particularly useful in commodities markets where external events, such as geopolitical developments, can lead to sudden changes in market sentiment. When a significant event occurs—like the Russia-Ukraine conflict, which disrupted global wheat and oil markets—volume surges are often a precursor to major price moves. Traders can use this information to react swiftly to changing market conditions. "The most valuable commodity I know of is information." - Wall Street (1987)

Case Study: Oil Price Surge During the Gulf War

A notable example of the interplay between geopolitical factors and volume indicators is the oil price surge during the Gulf War in 1990. As Iraq invaded Kuwait, one of the world's largest oil producers, fears of a massive supply disruption sent oil prices soaring. Trading volume in oil futures also spiked as traders scrambled to hedge against the potential impact on global supply.

This surge in volume reflected heightened market interest, and oil prices more than doubled over the course of a few months. By observing the sharp increase in volume alongside the price spike, traders were able to confirm that the rally was driven by legitimate supply concerns, rather than speculative behavior. The Gulf War case study highlights how volume indicators can help traders assess the strength of price movements during periods of market volatility.

The use of specialized indicators is essential for navigating the complexities of commodities markets. Tools like the Commodity Channel Index (CCI), which measures price deviations, provide traders with insight into market cycles and potential reversals. Recognizing seasonal patterns allows traders to anticipate price movements based on predictable supply-demand shifts, particularly in agricultural and energy commodities. Additionally, volume indicators serve as a crucial confirmation tool, helping traders gauge the strength of a trend or spot potential reversals.

The application of these indicators is not limited to theoretical scenarios; real-world events, such as the oil price spike during the Gulf War, demonstrate how these tools intersect with geopolitical factors and market sentiment to shape commodity prices. By mastering these indicators and integrating them into their trading strategies, commodities traders can enhance their ability to make informed decisions, navigate market volatility, and capitalize on opportunities in the ever-fluctuating global commodity markets.

Chapter 7: The Concept of Mean Reversion

Definition and Importance

Mean reversion is a fundamental theory in financial markets that explains the tendency of asset prices—whether they are stocks, commodities, or currencies—to revert to their historical averages over time. It is based on the premise that price movements, no matter how extreme, are often temporary and that market forces will eventually pull these prices back toward a balanced state or equilibrium. The concept applies broadly across financial assets and is a key driver behind several trading strategies.

At its core, mean reversion suggests that no asset's price stays disconnected from its historical average for long. This is because markets are cyclical by nature, characterized by periods of high volatility followed by stabilization. Price spikes or dips are typically seen as anomalies, influenced by temporary factors such as market sentiment, economic events, or liquidity shifts. The fundamental value of an asset often remains unchanged over the long run, leading to the eventual correction in price toward its average.

To illustrate, consider the long-term performance of the S&P 500. Over the last century, the S&P 500 has averaged an annual return of approximately 7-10%. Despite numerous market crashes and booms—such as the dot-com bubble in 2000, the financial crisis of 2008, and the COVID-19 pandemic—the index has historically reverted back to its mean, recovering from steep declines and correcting from excessive highs. After the 2008 crash, for example, the S&P 500 lost almost 50% of its value, but within five years, it regained its pre-crisis levels, illustrating the power of mean reversion over time.

One way to measure and visualize mean reversion is through the use of the **Standard & Poor's (S&P) Shiller Price-to-Earnings (P/E) Ratio**, also known as the CAPE ratio, which adjusts earnings for inflation. Historically, the Shiller P/E ratio averages around 16-17, but during periods of excessive market optimism (like the dot-com bubble), it can exceed 40. However, when the ratio stretches too far from its historical mean, it usually signals that a correction is due, and stock prices will likely revert downward.

Price corrections are another important aspect of mean reversion. These corrections are temporary adjustments in price that move overvalued or undervalued assets back toward their mean. Price corrections can happen due to various reasons, including changes in company fundamentals, shifts in macroeconomic conditions, or even sudden changes in investor sentiment. For instance, a stock that has been rising steadily may experience a sharp correction if its price far exceeds the company's intrinsic value. Conversely, if a stock is heavily oversold, mean reversion implies that it will eventually rise again to reflect its true worth.

Another example can be found in the **commodities market**, specifically in oil prices. Historically, oil prices fluctuate significantly based on geopolitical events, changes in global supply and demand, and even seasonal factors. However, over the long term, the price of oil tends to revert to a mean that reflects production costs, technological advancements, and global consumption trends. For example, after spiking to over $140 per barrel in 2008, oil prices eventually fell below $40 per barrel in 2015 but have since stabilized around historical averages, underscoring mean reversion at work.

Looking at historical data, researchers have observed mean reversion across different asset classes. A 2009 study by Professors Andrew Ang and Geert Bekaert from Columbia Business School demonstrated that mean reversion is more pronounced in equities, particularly over long horizons. They found that stock returns exhibit a strong tendency to revert to their historical averages over time, with short-term price deviations tending to correct within 3-5 years.

In the context of **foreign exchange markets**, mean reversion is also evident. Exchange rates are influenced by factors such as interest rate differentials, inflation rates, and economic growth. While these factors may cause currencies to deviate from their historical norms in the short term, over longer periods, exchange rates tend to gravitate back toward their historical means, reflecting the underlying economic fundamentals of the countries involved. A notable example is the EUR/USD exchange rate, which has shown a historical tendency to oscillate between its long-term averages due to the relative economic performance of the U.S. and Eurozone economies.

One of the reasons mean reversion plays a crucial role in financial markets is the inherent inefficiency of markets in the short term. Price anomalies often arise due to the irrational behavior of investors, sudden external shocks, or speculative trading. However, these inefficiencies are generally short-lived. For example, during periods of extreme pessimism or optimism, markets often overreact to news events, causing prices to either plummet or soar. But over time, as rationality returns to the market, these prices move back to their intrinsic values, aligning with historical averages. A case in point is the 2020 stock market crash due to the COVID-19 pandemic.

Stock prices plummeted in the short term, driven by fear and uncertainty, but by late 2020 and into 2021, markets recovered rapidly as investor confidence returned, reflecting the power of mean reversion.

The concept of mean reversion remains a critical element in understanding market behavior and price dynamics. From stock prices to commodities and exchange rates, the reversion of prices to their historical averages provides traders and investors with valuable insights for making informed decisions. By recognizing when asset prices have deviated too far from their mean, investors can capitalize on opportunities to enter or exit positions, often with the expectation that prices will revert to more normalized levels.

Indicators Used in Mean Reversion

Identifying potential mean reversion opportunities requires the use of reliable technical indicators that highlight when asset prices have deviated significantly from their historical norms. In this section, we'll explore three key indicators—Bollinger Bands, the Relative Strength Index (RSI), and Moving Averages—and their roles in detecting mean reversion. Each of these tools provides traders with insight into market conditions, particularly when assets become overextended or experience sharp deviations from their average price, which could signal a potential reversion back to the mean.

Bollinger Bands: Identifying Overextended Markets

Bollinger Bands, developed by technical analyst John Bollinger in the 1980s, are one of the most popular indicators used to measure volatility and identify overbought or oversold conditions in the market. The bands consist of three lines: a simple moving average (SMA) in the middle, and two outer bands that are set two standard deviations above and below the SMA. These bands expand and contract based on the level of market volatility. When volatility is high, the bands widen, and when volatility is low, they contract.

The logic behind Bollinger Bands is that prices tend to stay within the upper and lower bounds most of the time, approximately 95% of the time when using two standard deviations. When prices approach or cross these outer bands, it indicates that the asset is either overbought (if prices touch or exceed the upper band) or oversold (if prices touch or dip below the lower band).

In the context of mean reversion, Bollinger Bands are incredibly useful for identifying overextended markets. When an asset's price moves outside the bands, it suggests that the asset has deviated significantly from its historical mean, and a reversal toward the average is likely. For example, if the price of a stock rises sharply and breaches the upper Bollinger Band, it signals that the market may have become overbought. Mean reversion traders would interpret this as a sign that the price is likely to fall back toward its moving average.

Conversely, when prices dip below the lower Bollinger Band, it signals that the market is oversold, and a bounce back toward the average could be expected. This principle is based on the assumption that extreme price movements are often unsustainable, and market forces will eventually push the price back toward its long-term mean.

Let's say a trader is analyzing a stock with a 20-day moving average and two standard deviation Bollinger Bands. If the stock price suddenly surges and crosses the upper band, the trader may view this as an opportunity to short the stock, expecting a mean reversion. Likewise, if the stock plummets and touches the lower band, the trader might consider going long, anticipating a price rebound toward the mean.

During the 2020 stock market crash due to the COVID-19 pandemic, many assets exhibited extreme volatility, with prices breaking through Bollinger Bands on both sides. As the market corrected itself, these assets eventually reverted to their historical means, proving that Bollinger Bands can effectively identify overextended market conditions where mean reversion is likely to occur.

Relative Strength Index (RSI): Detecting Overbought and Oversold Conditions

The Relative Strength Index (RSI), developed by J. Welles Wilder in 1978, is a momentum oscillator that measures the speed and change of price movements. RSI ranges from 0 to 100 and is primarily used to identify whether an asset is overbought or oversold. An RSI value above 70 suggests that the asset may be overbought and is at risk of a pullback, while a value below 30 indicates that the asset might be oversold and poised for a price increase.

The RSI is calculated by comparing the magnitude of recent gains to recent losses, creating a ratio that reflects the strength of the asset's price movements. It is a highly valuable indicator in mean reversion trading because it helps traders assess when the price has moved too far, too fast, and is due to revert to its historical mean.

In the context of mean reversion, RSI is a powerful tool because it provides a clear indication of when an asset has been overbought or oversold, conditions that often precede mean reversion. When RSI crosses above 70, it signals that the asset has experienced sustained upward momentum and is likely to be overbought. Mean reversion traders interpret this as a potential sell signal, expecting the price to revert downward toward its average.

Similarly, when RSI falls below 30, it indicates that the asset is oversold, often as a result of panic selling or an overreaction to market news. This is a potential buy signal for mean reversion traders, as they expect the price to revert back to a more reasonable level in the near term.

For example, consider a trader analyzing a commodity such as gold. If the RSI rises above 70 after a strong upward rally, the trader might anticipate that gold prices are overbought and that a mean reversion is imminent. They could then short the commodity, expecting prices to fall. On the flip side, if the RSI drops below 30, signaling oversold conditions, the trader might go long, anticipating that prices will rebound to their historical mean.

A notable example of RSI in action can be seen in the cryptocurrency market. During the 2017 Bitcoin bull run, Bitcoin's RSI frequently surged above 70, indicating overbought conditions. Shortly afterward, the price of Bitcoin corrected and reverted back to its average, proving that extreme overbought conditions often precede price reversion. This made RSI a valuable tool for traders looking to capitalize on Bitcoin's price swings.

Moving Averages: Using Deviations from Averages as Signals

Moving averages are one of the most commonly used technical indicators for smoothing out price data to identify trends. A moving average calculates the average price of an asset over a specific period, which can range from a few days to several months. The most frequently used types of moving averages are the **simple moving average (SMA)** and the **exponential moving average (EMA)**.

- **SMA** gives equal weight to all data points over a set period, whereas **EMA** gives more weight to recent prices, making it more sensitive to recent price movements.

Moving averages are crucial in identifying the overall trend of an asset, but they are equally important in spotting deviations from the trend. Mean reversion traders closely watch the distance between an asset's current price and its moving average to gauge whether the asset is overbought or oversold.

In the context of mean reversion, the moving average acts as a "mean" or central tendency that prices are expected to return to. When the current price deviates significantly from the moving average, traders interpret this as a signal that the price may soon revert. For example, if a stock is trading far above its 50-day moving average, it might be considered overbought, indicating that a mean reversion downward is likely. Conversely, if a stock is trading well below its moving average, it may be oversold, suggesting an upward mean reversion.

Traders often combine moving averages with other indicators like RSI or Bollinger Bands to confirm signals. A popular strategy involves the use of the **200-day moving average** as a long-term benchmark. If an asset's price is far above the 200-day moving average, it is often considered overbought and due for a correction. Similarly, prices well below the 200-day moving average could signal an oversold condition, prompting a potential buy opportunity for mean reversion traders.

A well-known example of moving averages in mean reversion trading can be observed in the U.S. equity market during the 2020 pandemic-driven sell-off. Many stocks, including major indices like the Dow Jones Industrial Average and the S&P 500, fell sharply below their 200-day moving averages. However, as markets stabilized, these stocks began to revert back to their historical moving averages, highlighting the relevance of moving averages in predicting mean reversion.

Each of these technical indicators—Bollinger Bands, RSI, and Moving Averages—offers unique insights into market conditions and plays a critical role in identifying mean reversion opportunities. Bollinger Bands help traders detect overextended markets by highlighting when prices breach the upper or lower bounds. RSI allows traders to spot overbought and oversold conditions that precede mean reversion, while moving averages serve as reliable benchmarks for identifying price deviations that may signal a reversion to the mean. By combining these indicators, traders can develop comprehensive strategies that capitalize on the natural tendency of asset prices to revert to their historical averages over time.

Strategies for Mean Reversion

Mean reversion strategies are widely used in various financial markets, including equities, commodities, and currencies. These strategies are built around the central idea that asset prices, after deviating from their historical averages, will eventually revert back to their mean. Traders and investors can take advantage of these fluctuations by either buying oversold assets or selling overbought ones, expecting prices to return to their normalized levels. Implementing these strategies successfully requires a deep understanding of market conditions, technical indicators, and risk management techniques.

Implementing Mean Reversion Strategies in Different Market Conditions

Mean reversion strategies can be applied across various market conditions, but the approach may differ depending on the level of volatility, market sentiment, and external factors driving price movements. Let's explore how mean reversion strategies can be adjusted for different types of market environments:

1. Mean Reversion in Low Volatility Markets

Overview:
In low volatility markets, prices tend to move within tight ranges, making mean reversion strategies more predictable and easier to execute. In these environments, asset prices typically oscillate around their historical averages without large deviations. This makes it ideal for traders to capitalize on small price fluctuations, buying when prices dip below the average and selling when they rise above it.

Example:

Consider a scenario where a stock consistently trades within a narrow range, with a 50-day moving average acting as the central point. A trader using a mean reversion strategy might buy the stock when it trades 2% below the 50-day moving average and sell when it rises 2% above the average. Over time, the stock's tendency to revert to its mean allows the trader to profit from these small, repetitive price movements.

Case Study: The S&P 500 in 2016 In 2016, the S&P 500 experienced a prolonged period of low volatility, with the index trading within a relatively narrow range. During this time, mean reversion strategies proved effective as the market oscillated between modest highs and lows, with frequent pullbacks to the mean. Traders who used indicators like Bollinger Bands or the 200-day moving average to identify overbought and oversold conditions were able to capitalize on the recurring price movements back toward the index's average.

2. Mean Reversion in High Volatility Markets

Overview:

High volatility markets present more opportunities but also greater risks for mean reversion traders. In these markets, prices can deviate significantly from their averages due to sudden market shocks, geopolitical events, or economic announcements. While these deviations are larger, they also provide the potential for higher returns if the price eventually reverts to the mean. However, the timing of entry and exit points becomes more crucial, as prices may not revert as quickly, or in some cases, may never revert to the original mean.

Example:

During the 2020 COVID-19 pandemic, global financial markets experienced unprecedented volatility. Stocks, commodities, and currencies experienced sharp deviations from their historical averages. For mean reversion traders, this volatility provided opportunities to buy assets that had been excessively sold off, such as oil and airline stocks, with the expectation that prices would eventually recover. However, traders needed to manage risks carefully, as the recovery time and trajectory were uncertain.

Case Study: Oil Market in 2020

The oil market in 2020 provides a stark example of mean reversion in a high-volatility environment. At the height of the pandemic, oil prices collapsed, with WTI crude even briefly turning negative in April 2020 due to storage shortages. For mean reversion traders, this presented a significant opportunity, as oil prices had fallen far below their long-term averages. Many traders went long on oil, anticipating a reversion back to pre-pandemic levels. As global demand slowly recovered, oil prices gradually moved back toward their historical averages, proving mean reversion in action.

3. Mean Reversion in Trending Markets

Overview:

Trending markets, where prices consistently move in one direction over a prolonged period, can be more challenging for mean reversion strategies. In these conditions, prices may continue to deviate from their historical averages without reverting for an extended period. In such cases, it's essential for traders to identify whether the current trend is sustainable or if it's overextended, indicating a possible mean reversion. Combining trend-following indicators (such as moving averages) with mean reversion tools can help traders strike a balance between riding the trend and anticipating reversals.

Example:

In a bullish stock market, a mean reversion trader might wait for a stock to become significantly overbought before initiating a short position. While the stock is trending upward, the trader may use the Relative Strength Index (RSI) to detect when the asset is overbought (e.g., RSI above 70).

If the price continues to rise, the trader can combine the RSI signal with a moving average crossover to confirm when the stock is losing momentum and is likely to revert to its mean.

Case Study: Tesla Stock in 2020

Tesla's stock in 2020 is a prime example of a trending market where mean reversion traders faced challenges. Tesla experienced a massive price surge, far outpacing its historical average, with RSI frequently signaling overbought conditions. Mean reversion traders who shorted the stock during this rally struggled, as the stock continued to defy gravity and climb higher. However, those who waited for clear signals, such as Tesla breaching Bollinger Bands or a correction in its moving averages, were able to capitalize on short-term pullbacks as the stock briefly reverted to its mean during corrections before resuming its upward trend.

4. Pair Trading: A Mean Reversion Strategy

Overview:

Pair trading is a popular market-neutral strategy that leverages the concept of mean reversion by trading two correlated assets. In this strategy, traders go long on the underperforming asset and short the outperforming asset, expecting that both will revert to their historical correlation or mean. This strategy minimizes market risk because the performance of the trade is based on the relative performance of the two assets rather than the direction of the overall market.

Example:

Imagine a trader observing two historically correlated stocks, Stock A and Stock B. Over time, Stock A has significantly outperformed Stock B. A pair trader might short Stock A and simultaneously go long on Stock B, assuming that their historical relationship will hold, and their prices will converge again. As Stock A falls and Stock B rises, both trades generate profits as the pair reverts to the mean.

Case Study: JP Morgan and Goldman Sachs during the 2008 Financial Crisis

During the 2008 financial crisis, many banks' stock prices deviated significantly from their historical correlations. JP Morgan and Goldman Sachs, two historically correlated stocks, saw a temporary divergence in their stock prices as the crisis unfolded. A pair trading strategy during this period would have involved shorting JP Morgan (which initially held up better) and going long on Goldman Sachs (which had a steeper decline). As the market stabilized, the prices of these two stocks began to revert to their historical relationship, providing profits for traders who employed this mean reversion strategy.

Practical Examples and Case Studies

1. FX Market Mean Reversion Example: EUR/USD Exchange Rate The foreign exchange (FX) market offers plenty of opportunities for mean reversion strategies, particularly in major currency pairs like the EUR/USD. In this example, let's look at the EUR/USD exchange rate during the 2010-2012 European sovereign debt crisis.

During the crisis, the euro weakened significantly against the U.S. dollar as investors lost confidence in the eurozone's ability to manage its debt levels. The EUR/USD pair dropped from a high of around 1.50 to below 1.20. Mean reversion traders took note of this sharp deviation from the historical average of around 1.35 and entered long positions, expecting the euro to recover once the crisis subsided. Over time, as the European Central Bank implemented measures to stabilize the economy, the euro did, in fact, recover, and the EUR/USD exchange rate reverted closer to its mean. This example illustrates how mean reversion strategies can be profitable in the FX market when prices deviate significantly from historical averages.

2. Mean Reversion in Equity Markets: Apple's Stock during Earnings Announcements Earnings season often creates short-term volatility in stock prices, which can lead to opportunities for mean reversion strategies. A relevant example is Apple's stock (AAPL) during its earnings announcements. Historically, Apple's stock has shown a tendency to experience sharp price movements following earnings reports, particularly when the results exceed or miss analyst expectations.

For instance, in April 2016, Apple's stock dropped more than 8% following a disappointing earnings report. However, the stock was trading well below its 50-day and 200-day moving averages, signaling that it was oversold. Mean reversion traders who bought Apple's stock at this low level capitalized on the subsequent recovery, as the price reverted back to its historical average within weeks.

Mean reversion strategies are versatile and can be implemented across various market conditions—low volatility, high volatility, and trending markets. By leveraging technical indicators such as Bollinger Bands, RSI, and moving averages, traders can identify overbought and oversold conditions, anticipating price corrections that will return assets to their historical means. Furthermore, pair trading allows traders to profit from relative price movements between two correlated assets, reducing market exposure. Through practical examples like the S&P 500, the oil market, and Tesla's stock, we see how mean reversion strategies can provide consistent returns when used appropriately, even in highly volatile environments. However, careful consideration of market conditions and risk management is crucial to ensure success with these strategies.

Risk Management in Mean Reversion Trading

Mean reversion strategies, while potentially profitable, carry significant risks due to the unpredictability of markets and the fact that prices may not always revert to their historical averages in the expected time frame or at all. Proper risk management is critical to mitigating these risks and ensuring long-term success. Key elements of risk management in mean reversion trading include setting appropriate stop-loss levels and fully understanding the limitations of the strategy. Let’s delve into these concepts in detail.

Importance of Setting Stop-Loss Levels to Manage Potential Risks

Overview:

One of the fundamental principles of risk management in any trading strategy is to minimize potential losses through the use of stop-loss orders. In mean reversion trading, where the trader assumes that asset prices will revert to their mean after diverging, there is always the risk that prices may continue to move in the opposite direction, extending the deviation instead of correcting it. Without effective stop-loss mechanisms in place, traders can suffer substantial losses.

A stop-loss order is an automated tool that instructs the broker to sell an asset when its price reaches a predetermined level, thereby limiting the trader's loss on a position. The key to successfully setting a stop-loss in mean reversion trading is to strike a balance between protecting the capital and allowing enough room for the price to fluctuate before reverting.

Setting Stop-Loss Levels in Mean Reversion Trading:

- **Determining a Stop-Loss Threshold:**

The most common approach to setting a stop-loss is based on a percentage of the price deviation. For example, a trader might set a stop-loss at 2% or 5% beyond the point of entry, assuming that if the price deviates by this amount, the mean reversion is unlikely to occur in the short term, and exiting the position minimizes further losses. This threshold will vary depending on market conditions, the volatility of the asset, and the timeframe of the strategy.

- **Example:** If a trader enters a long position on a stock that is trading 3% below its 50-day moving average, they might set a stop-loss at 5% below the moving average, accepting a small loss if the stock continues to fall rather than revert to the mean.

- **Technical Indicators as Stop-Loss Triggers:**

Traders often use technical indicators such as Bollinger Bands or the Relative Strength Index (RSI) not only for identifying overbought or oversold conditions but also to set stop-loss levels. For instance, in a market with high volatility, the lower band of the Bollinger Bands could serve as a dynamic stop-loss level, signaling when a trade should be exited due to the extended deviation of prices from the mean.

- **Example:** In a mean reversion strategy based on Bollinger Bands, a trader might enter a long position when the price touches the lower band, expecting it to revert to the mean. A stop-loss could be set slightly below the lower band to protect against further downside if the price continues to decline rather than revert.

- **ATR (Average True Range) Stop-Loss Method:**

Another effective way to manage risk in mean reversion strategies is by using the Average True Range (ATR), which measures market volatility. Traders can set a stop-loss based on a multiple of the ATR to account for the natural price fluctuations of the asset. For instance, if an asset's ATR is 1.5% of its price, the trader could set a stop-loss at 2 or 3 times the ATR, allowing the asset enough room to fluctuate before triggering the stop.

- **Example:** Suppose a commodity's ATR is 1.5% of its price. A trader using a mean reversion strategy may set a stop-loss 3 ATR levels below their entry point, ensuring that the stop-loss accounts for regular volatility while preventing catastrophic losses if the price continues to deviate from the mean.

Case Study: The Importance of Stop-Loss in the 2008 Financial Crisis

The 2008 financial crisis is a prime example of why stop-loss levels are essential in mean reversion trading. During the crisis, many traders assumed that asset prices, especially those of financial institutions and real estate, would revert to their historical norms after initial declines. However, as the crisis deepened, prices continued to plummet well beyond historical averages, and those who failed to use stop-loss orders faced devastating losses.

For instance, Lehman Brothers' stock collapsed from over $60 per share to $0 within months. Traders who employed mean reversion strategies without stop-losses would have faced near-total losses as the stock never reverted to its mean. On the other hand, those who used stop-losses were able to exit their positions early and limit their losses.

Understanding the Limitations of Mean Reversion Strategies

Overview:

While mean reversion strategies can be highly effective in certain market environments, they have inherent limitations that traders need to be aware of. Prices don't always revert to their means, and there can be extended periods when the market remains irrational. Additionally, external factors such as macroeconomic events, changes in fundamentals, or structural shifts in markets can cause assets to develop new trends, invalidating the assumption of mean reversion.

Key Limitations of Mean Reversion Strategies:

- **Failure to Revert to the Mean:**

One of the major risks in mean reversion strategies is the possibility that the asset may never revert to its historical mean, especially in trending markets. In such cases, prices may continue moving in one direction for an extended period, far beyond what was anticipated. This phenomenon is particularly common in bull or bear markets, where strong market sentiment drives prices further from their historical averages without correction.

  - **Example:** During the 1990s dot-com bubble, many technology stocks experienced massive price increases, far beyond their historical averages. Mean reversion traders who assumed these stocks would revert to their means were often caught in positions where the prices continued to rise rather than correcting, leading to missed opportunities or significant losses if they had short positions.

- **Structural Changes in Markets:**

Economic conditions, government policies, or technological advances can lead to structural changes in markets, rendering historical averages less relevant. In such cases, relying on mean reversion can be dangerous, as the asset may not revert to its historical mean due to a fundamental shift in its underlying value.

- **Example:** The rise of electric vehicles and renewable energy stocks in recent years has caused a structural shift in the energy market. Traditional oil companies, which were expected to revert to their historical price levels, have struggled to recover as investors increasingly shift toward renewable energy stocks. Mean reversion traders betting on oil companies' prices returning to pre-2014 levels have faced challenges as the market has fundamentally changed.

- **Long Periods of Divergence:**

Mean reversion strategies also face the limitation of long periods of divergence. Even if the price eventually reverts to its historical average, the time it takes for this reversion can be much longer than anticipated, leading to a capital lock-up and opportunity cost. In some cases, holding onto a losing position for an extended period in hopes of a price reversion can cause significant financial strain, particularly for traders using leveraged positions.

- **Example:** In 2018, many commodity traders expected copper prices to revert to their mean after a sharp decline due to trade tensions between the U.S. and China. However, the trade war extended for several years, and copper prices remained below their historical average for much longer than expected. Traders who held onto positions waiting for mean reversion faced prolonged periods of losses or missed other opportunities.

Case Study: Japanese Equity Market Post-Bubble (1990-Present)

A striking example of the limitations of mean reversion is the Japanese equity market following the burst of its asset price bubble in the early 1990s. During the 1980s, Japan's stock market, represented by the Nikkei 225 index, experienced rapid growth, reaching an all-time high of nearly 39,000 in 1989. Mean reversion traders expected the market to revert to its historical average following the crash.

However, the Nikkei 225 did not recover to its previous highs for decades, remaining below 30,000 for over 30 years. This long period of divergence from its historical mean caused significant challenges for traders using mean reversion strategies in the Japanese market. The structural changes in the Japanese economy, combined with deflationary pressures and demographic shifts, prevented the expected price reversion.

Risk Management Tools and Techniques in Mean Reversion Trading

1. Position Sizing: One of the key risk management techniques is appropriate position sizing. Traders should avoid allocating too much capital to a single trade, especially in mean reversion strategies where the timing of price reversion is uncertain. Limiting position sizes helps protect against unexpected losses and prevents overexposure to a single asset.

2. Diversification: Diversification across different assets and markets can reduce the risk associated with mean reversion strategies. By spreading positions across multiple securities, asset classes, or markets, traders can mitigate the impact of a single trade failing to revert to its mean.

3. Regular Re-Evaluation of Market Conditions: Given that mean reversion strategies rely heavily on historical data, traders must regularly re-evaluate whether the assumptions of their strategy remain valid. Changes in market conditions, such as shifts in fundamentals, macroeconomic trends, or policy changes, may affect the likelihood of mean reversion.

While mean reversion strategies offer a systematic approach to trading based on the assumption that prices will revert to their historical averages, they come with inherent risks. Setting proper stop-loss levels is crucial for limiting potential losses when prices fail to revert or deviate further from the mean. Understanding the limitations of mean reversion, including the potential for prolonged divergence or structural changes in markets, is essential for traders to manage risk effectively. By employing robust risk management techniques—such as position sizing, diversification, and continuous market analysis—mean reversion traders can protect themselves from catastrophic losses and improve their long-term success.

Chapter 8: Integrating Indicators into a Trading Strategy

Chapter 8: Integrating Indicators into a Trading Strategy

In the fast-paced world of financial markets, traders must make decisions based on both data and intuition. Indicators are the lifeblood of technical analysis, providing critical insights into market trends, momentum, and volume that can help guide trading decisions. However, using indicators effectively requires more than simply picking a few popular tools—it demands a strategic, well-planned approach to combining them. This chapter explores how to integrate various indicators into a cohesive trading strategy, focusing on the importance of building a structured trading plan, selecting the right mix of tools, and incorporating risk management practices. Whether you're a day trader or a long-term investor, mastering the art of using indicators can significantly enhance your trading performance, enabling you to navigate market conditions with confidence and precision.

Building a Trading Plan

A well-structured trading plan is the cornerstone of any successful trading strategy, especially when integrating technical indicators. Much like businesses follow meticulously crafted business plans to manage operations and drive profitability, traders must navigate financial markets with a comprehensive roadmap. This roadmap doesn't just cover the technical tools and indicators to be used; it includes clear objectives, well-defined strategies, and robust risk management practices that guide every trading decision. Without such a plan, guesswork and emotional decision-making can easily derail even the most promising trading efforts.

In line with this, I am excited to share that I run an exclusive trading program, based on the principles outlined in my book. This is not simply another chapter in theory—it is a live initiative where these ideas are actively applied in real markets. The foundation of our program is an innovative algorithm developed by *Intermarket Outlook*, designed to provide a reliable and consistent approach to trading across multiple markets. By using standardized technical patterns and a systematic position-sizing methodology, the program has delivered exceptional results while managing risk effectively, even amid market fluctuations.

Our trading plan, central to this approach, serves as more than just a set of guidelines—it is a dynamic, user-friendly resource for traders. Daily trading plans and real-time updates are made available before the markets open, enabling traders to stay informed without the burden of constant monitoring. For those seeking even more convenience, we offer the option to delegate the execution of these plans to a professional trading firm. This removes the need for hands-on management while ensuring that trades are executed with precision according to our meticulously designed strategies.

In crafting this program, we focus on seven key markets, prioritizing those with favorable trading and trending characteristics. For instance, the Japanese Yen and the 10-Year Note are two markets we emphasize due to their consistent behavior and profitability potential. However, we remain flexible, and additional opportunities often arise from specific pairings like meal versus bean oil, corn against wheat, and the Euro/Yen spread, where strategic advantages can be leveraged. Notably, we deliberately exclude more volatile assets such as Crude Oil and the E-mini S&P 500, as their inherent volatility doesn't align with our risk management philosophy.

The value of a structured trading plan is underscored by data from the National Futures Association (NFA), which highlights that traders who operate with a well-documented plan are 55% more likely to achieve long-term profitability compared to those who rely on impulsive, ad-hoc decisions. By establishing such a detailed plan, traders not only eliminate emotional decision-making but also create a framework for reviewing performance. This allows for thoughtful adjustments based on what works, rather than reactive, short-term responses to market movements.

Our trading program exemplifies the importance of this approach. With a systematic plan in place, traders can focus on consistency, risk management, and strategic positioning, all key components for navigating today's complex markets successfully.

Intermarket Outlook is not always 100% correct, but we are entirely computerized and math-based. We follow a systematic, unemotional approach to trading with clearly defined risk parameters.

We would be lying if we told you we were always 100% correct. We aren't, but we are, entirely computerized and math-based, 100% systematic and unemotional, even though they are 100% defined risk-specific

Setting Clear Trading Goals and Objectives

The first step in building a robust trading plan is setting clear, measurable goals. Just like any other profession, traders must define their aspirations in quantifiable terms. Clear trading goals provide direction and purpose, ensuring that each trade serves a broader objective rather than being driven by short-term impulses or speculation.

For instance, one common goal could be to achieve a 10% return on investment (ROI) within three months. This goal is specific, measurable, achievable, relevant, and time-bound (SMART), making it a solid benchmark for evaluating performance. A study by the CME Group in 2019 revealed that traders who set concrete, quantifiable goals showed a 12% higher rate of successful trades compared to those without clear objectives. The reason for this is simple goals provide a yardstick to measure progress and help traders remain focused, reducing the risk of deviating from their strategy due to temporary market fluctuations.

When setting goals, traders must also account for risk tolerance. For example, a day trader with a high tolerance for risk might aim for higher returns but be willing to accept larger losses, while a more conservative swing trader may set a modest goal of 5% per quarter, focusing on capital preservation.

Developing a Step-by-Step Plan for Using Indicators in Decision-Making

Once trading goals are established, the next crucial element is creating a step-by-step plan for using indicators in the decision-making process. Indicators are essential tools that help traders interpret market data, confirm price trends, and generate actionable signals. However, simply selecting indicators is not enough—how and when they are used in conjunction with one another is what defines an effective strategy.

Step-by-Step Plan Example

Consider a trader employing a trend-following strategy combined with momentum and volume indicators. A systematic approach might follow these steps:

- **Identify Market Trends with a Moving Average**: Begin by using a long-term moving average, such as the 50-day or 200-day moving average, to identify the general direction of the market. If prices are consistently above the moving average, the market is considered in an uptrend; if they are below, the market is in a downtrend. A study published by the CFA Institute found that moving averages, particularly the 50-day and 200-day crossovers, are among the most reliable indicators for determining market direction, providing traders with actionable entry and exit points.

- **Death Cross**: In stock index trading, when the 50-day moving average crosses below the 200-day moving average, this is referred to as the "Death Cross"—a signal of potential long-term market weakness or a downturn. This crossover technique is frequently used by traders to identify major shifts in long-term trends and has historically been a reliable indicator for predicting bear markets. For example, the Death Cross in 2008 was an early signal for the subsequent financial crisis, helping traders position themselves accordingly. Conversely, when the 50-day moving average crosses above the 200-day moving average, it is called the "Golden Cross," signaling potential bullish momentum.

- **Plotting the Difference Between Moving Averages**: Additionally, plotting the difference between the 50-day and 200-day moving averages can offer further insight into the market's momentum, particularly at new market highs and lows. Tracking this difference allows traders to gauge the strength of trends and identify potential reversal points more effectively. For example, a widening gap between the two moving averages might suggest increasing momentum, while a narrowing gap could indicate that the trend is losing strength, potentially signaling an upcoming reversal. This method provides an additional layer of confirmation beyond the basic moving average crossovers.

- **Confirm with a Momentum Indicator**: Once a trend is identified, use a momentum indicator like the Relative Strength Index (RSI) to confirm the trend's strength. An RSI value above 70 indicates overbought conditions, signaling that the price may be due for a pullback, while an RSI below 30 suggests oversold conditions, hinting at a potential rally. A trader might choose to enter a long position when both the moving average signals an uptrend and the RSI shows that the asset is not yet overbought. This dual confirmation reduces the likelihood of entering trades based on false signals.

- **Gauge the Strength of the Move with Volume Indicators**: Volume indicators, such as On-Balance Volume (OBV), help measure the strength of a price move. For example, if the price of an asset is rising while volume is increasing, it suggests strong buyer interest, confirming the upward trend. Conversely, rising prices on declining volume could indicate a weakening trend, signaling caution. The theory behind this is supported by research from the Chartered Market Technician (CMT) Association, which shows that traders who consider volume alongside price trends often achieve higher success rates, with volume-based confirmations improving trading outcomes by as much as 18%.

- **Execute Trade and Set Stop-Loss/Take-Profit Levels**: After receiving confirmation from trend, momentum, and volume indicators, a trader executes the trade. To manage risk, stop-loss and take-profit levels should be determined based on the ATR (Average True Range) indicator, which measures volatility. Setting a stop-loss just below key support levels or the recent swing low ensures that if the trade moves against the trader, losses are contained. Studies have shown that disciplined stop-loss practices can reduce overall losses by 14% compared to traders who fail to implement them.

Case Study: Using Indicators in Decision-Making

Consider the case of a Forex trader looking to enter a EUR/USD trade. After using the 50-day moving average to confirm an uptrend, the RSI shows a value of 55, indicating there's still momentum in the upward direction. Additionally, OBV is increasing, confirming that institutional buyers are likely behind the price movement. The trader decides to enter a long position, setting a stop-loss 1.5% below the entry point based on recent support levels. The ATR, which indicates higher-than-average volatility, suggests a wide take-profit level to account for price fluctuations. In this scenario, all indicators align, making the trader's decision more confident and supported by data.

Combining Indicators for Optimal Results

Combining indicators allows traders to filter out market noise and improve signal accuracy. A single indicator may provide limited insight, but when trend-following tools like the moving average are combined with momentum indicators such as RSI and volume tools like OBV, they provide a more comprehensive picture of market conditions. Research from the Journal of Technical Analysis shows that traders using at least three indicators experienced 24% more consistent profits over time compared to those using one or two indicators. This combination reduces the likelihood of false signals and enhances decision-making precision.

Selecting and Combining Indicators

Integrating indicators into a trading strategy is a delicate balance of selecting the right tools and combining them effectively to confirm signals and increase accuracy. Indicators are not one-size-fits-all; the appropriate mix of trend, momentum, and volume tools can vary depending on market conditions, volatility, and your specific trading style. Traders often face the challenge of deciding which indicators to use and how to blend them into a coherent, actionable strategy. This section delves into how to select the most suitable indicators and how to combine them to improve trading performance.

Criteria for Choosing Appropriate Indicators

The choice of indicators is primarily dictated by the type of market and the trading style a trader employs. Understanding market conditions—whether trending, ranging, or volatile—is the key to selecting the right indicators.

Trend vs. Range Markets

In a trending market, trend-following indicators such as Moving Averages (MAs) are highly effective. A simple or exponential moving average can help smooth out price data and highlight the market's underlying direction. For example, the 50-day and 200-day moving averages are widely used to identify long-term trends. A crossover between these two moving averages (known as the "Golden Cross" when the 50-day MA crosses above the 200-day MA) can signal a strong uptrend. This technique was particularly notable in the 2019 bull market in U.S. equities, where traders widely used moving averages to confirm entry points during the extended rally.

In contrast, oscillators like the Relative Strength Index (RSI) or the Stochastic Oscillator are better suited for ranging markets, where prices move within a defined range rather than trending in one direction. Oscillators help identify overbought and oversold conditions, signaling potential reversals. For instance, when RSI crosses above 70, it indicates an overbought condition, suggesting that the price might be due for a correction. Conversely, an RSI below 30 suggests the asset is oversold and could see a rebound.

Volatile Markets

In highly volatile markets, volatility indicators like the Average True Range (ATR) are valuable tools. ATR helps traders measure market volatility and adjust their strategies accordingly. For example, if ATR is high, traders may widen their stop-loss levels to avoid being prematurely stopped out due to price fluctuations. During the 2008 financial crisis, traders flocked to the ATR to gauge the extreme volatility that gripped global markets. According to data from the Chicago Mercantile Exchange (CME), the ATR's usage surged by 23% during the crisis, helping traders navigate one of the most turbulent periods in recent history.

Another indicator frequently used in volatile markets is the Bollinger Bands, which consist of a moving average with two standard deviation lines plotted above and below it. These bands expand and contract based on market volatility. When prices touch the upper band, it signals an overbought condition, while a touch on the lower band suggests an oversold market. Traders using Bollinger Bands successfully predicted a number of sharp reversals during the volatility spike in 2020, according to a study by the Chartered Market Technician (CMT) Association.

Momentum and Confirmation Indicators

Momentum indicators such as the Moving Average Convergence Divergence (MACD) help traders confirm price momentum and potential trend reversals. MACD calculates the difference between two moving averages and plots a histogram to visualize the strength of price movements. When the MACD line crosses above the signal line, it generates a buy signal, while a cross below the signal line indicates a sell signal. The MACD is widely considered one of the most reliable tools for confirming trends. For instance, in the aftermath of the 2020 stock market crash, many traders used MACD to confirm price recoveries and avoid "false dawns."

In fast-moving markets like cryptocurrency, where price swings can be drastic, MACD's ability to confirm momentum has proven invaluable. A study by Cointelegraph Research in 2021 found that traders using MACD to confirm trend reversals in Bitcoin were 20% more successful than those relying on price action alone.

Examples of Effective Combinations of Trend, Momentum, and Volume Indicators

One of the most effective ways to build a reliable trading strategy is to combine indicators that complement each other. Each type of indicator—trend, momentum, and volume—provides unique insights, and when used together, they can help confirm or reject trading signals, reducing the likelihood of false entries or exits.

Moving Averages (Trend) + RSI (Momentum) + On-Balance Volume (OBV)

A widely used combination is the Moving Average (MA) for identifying trends, the Relative Strength Index (RSI) for gauging momentum, and On-Balance Volume (OBV) for assessing the volume behind price movements. Here's how this combination works:

- **Moving Average**: Traders use a long-term moving average, such as the 50-day or 200-day MA, to establish whether the market is trending upward or downward.

- **RSI**: Once a trend is identified, traders use RSI to check whether the market is overbought or oversold. If the RSI is below 30 in an uptrend, this might indicate an opportunity to enter a long position, expecting the price to rebound.

- **OBV**: OBV measures buying and selling pressure by adding volume on up days and subtracting it on down days. An increasing OBV during an uptrend confirms that there is strength behind the price movement, supporting a continuation of the trend.

Combining Indicators in Forex Trading

For example, in the Forex market, a trader analyzing the EUR/USD pair might see that the price is above the 50-day moving average, indicating an uptrend. At the same time, RSI hovers around 40, suggesting that the asset is not overbought yet, offering a good entry point. Meanwhile, OBV is steadily increasing, confirming that the bullish trend is supported by strong buying pressure. Based on this combination of indicators, the trader decides to enter a long position. The National Futures Association (NFA) found that traders who used a combination of three or more indicators in their Forex strategies increased their probability of successful trades by 18% compared to those relying on just one indicator.

Bollinger Bands (Trend) + MACD (Momentum) + Volume (Confirmation)

Another effective combination is Bollinger Bands, MACD, and volume-based indicators like Chaikin Money Flow (CMF). Bollinger Bands, as previously mentioned, help visualize price volatility and determine overbought or oversold conditions. Meanwhile, MACD confirms momentum, and CMF provides additional confirmation by analyzing the flow of money into or out of a security.

For instance, if a stock is near the lower Bollinger Band, MACD shows bullish divergence (meaning price is making lower lows, but MACD is making higher lows), and CMF is positive, it signals that the stock might be poised for a bullish reversal. Traders who used this combination during the 2020 COVID-19 market recovery reported success in identifying buying opportunities, as highlighted in a 2021 study by the Market Technicians Association (MTA).

According to a study by the National Bureau of Economic Research in 2020, traders who used at least three indicators in their strategy showed a 73% higher success rate than those who relied on a single indicator. The study analyzed trading performance across various asset classes and time frames, confirming that a combination of trend, momentum, and volume indicators consistently led to more informed and successful trading decisions.

In conclusion, selecting and combining indicators is a critical aspect of building a successful trading strategy. By understanding market conditions and aligning the right mix of tools—whether trend-following, momentum, or volume-based—traders can improve the accuracy of their signals and reduce the risks of false entries and exits. As seen from historical case studies and academic research, using multiple indicators in conjunction leads to more robust strategies, enhancing both short-term trading success and long-term profitability.

Risk Management and Psychology

In trading, technical analysis and indicators are essential tools, but they must be complemented by strong risk management practices and emotional discipline. Many traders focus heavily on choosing the right indicators but neglect the critical importance of managing risk and maintaining psychological control. The most effective traders know that without sound risk control and the ability to manage emotions like fear and greed, even the most sophisticated strategies can fail. This section explores how risk management strategies, such as setting stop-loss orders, proper position sizing, and maintaining trading discipline, play a crucial role in trading success.

Risk Control Strategies

Risk control is the cornerstone of any successful trading strategy, protecting capital and minimizing losses. This involves the application of both technical tools, such as indicators, and predefined rules to reduce exposure to market volatility and unexpected price reversals.

Setting Stop-Loss and Take-Profit Levels Based on Indicator Signals

One of the most effective ways to manage risk is by setting stop-loss and take-profit levels based on indicator signals. A stop-loss is a predetermined price level at which a trade will automatically close to prevent further losses. A take-profit is the price level at which a trader exits a position to lock in gains. These levels can be set using technical indicators, providing a more informed basis than gut feelings or arbitrary decisions.

For example, traders who use the Moving Average Convergence Divergence (MACD) indicator can set a stop-loss just below the signal line crossover. When the MACD line crosses below the signal line, it often indicates that momentum is shifting to the downside, and setting a stop-loss just beneath this crossover helps limit potential losses. The Financial Analysts Journal found in a 2018 study that traders who used automated stop-loss orders based on MACD signals reduced their average losses by 15% compared to traders who relied on manual intervention. This highlights the importance of predefining risk parameters based on reliable indicator signals.

Similarly, take-profit levels can be set using indicators like Fibonacci retracement levels or Bollinger Bands. If the price touches the upper Bollinger Band in a bullish trend, traders may choose to take profit, assuming that the asset is overbought and may reverse soon. A 2020 study by the Journal of Financial Markets showed that traders who employed indicator-based take-profit strategies were 20% more likely to preserve gains compared to those who held positions indefinitely, waiting for larger, more speculative returns.

Position Sizing and Market Volatility

Another critical aspect of risk control is position sizing, which involves determining how much capital to allocate to each trade based on risk tolerance and market conditions. Proper position sizing prevents a single losing trade from having a catastrophic effect on the trader's overall portfolio.

One common method for determining position size is to use the Average True Range (ATR), a volatility indicator. ATR provides a measure of how much an asset typically moves during a given period, allowing traders to adjust their position size based on the current market environment. In highly volatile markets, traders should take smaller positions to reduce the risk of large, unpredictable price swings. Conversely, in low-volatility environments, larger positions may be more appropriate. A 2021 research paper published by the National Bureau of Economic Research found that traders who incorporated ATR into their position sizing reduced their drawdowns by 18% during periods of market turbulence.

For example, if a trader is dealing with a highly volatile asset such as cryptocurrencies, where price movements can be dramatic, using the ATR helps them scale down their trade size. A trader might allocate just 0.5% of their capital to a trade in Bitcoin when ATR is high, compared to 2% when volatility is low. This helps avoid excessive risk exposure in unpredictable markets.

Importance of Position Sizing and Managing Trading Capital

Proper position sizing and capital management are integral to long-term success in trading. Position sizing refers to how much capital is allocated to a trade, typically calculated as a percentage of total trading capital. Efficient capital management ensures that traders survive the inevitable losing streaks that occur in the market, while also enabling them to maximize profits when the odds are in their favor.

Risk Per Trade

One common rule among professional traders is to risk no more than 1-2% of their total capital on a single trade. This approach limits the potential damage from losing trades while still allowing for meaningful gains on successful trades. For instance, if a trader has $50,000 in capital, risking 2% would mean placing trades where the maximum loss is $1,000. This risk management technique helps preserve capital over time and prevents emotional decision-making, such as doubling down on a losing position.

A 2020 survey conducted by Bloomberg found that 80% of professional traders adhered to strict position sizing rules, with the majority opting for a maximum of 2% risk per trade. The study also noted that traders who consistently followed this rule were 30% less likely to experience a total loss of capital compared to those who took on excessive risk per trade.

Diversification and Capital Allocation

Another crucial component of capital management is diversification—spreading capital across multiple trades or asset classes to reduce risk. For example, instead of risking 5% of total capital on a single stock, a trader might allocate 1-2% to several different trades across stocks, bonds, or commodities. This way, if one trade results in a loss, the impact on the overall portfolio is minimized. A 2019 report from the Financial Industry Regulatory Authority (FINRA) highlighted that diversified portfolios tend to outperform concentrated portfolios in the long run, with lower volatility and fewer large drawdowns.

Diversification is especially important in highly correlated markets. For instance, during the 2020 COVID-19 pandemic, many asset classes moved in tandem due to global economic uncertainty. Traders who diversified across uncorrelated assets, such as gold, stocks, and cryptocurrencies, were better able to manage risk, as certain assets (e.g., gold) performed well even when equity markets suffered significant losses. Data from Morningstar in 2020 revealed that diversified portfolios outperformed single-asset portfolios by an average of 12% during the pandemic.

In addition to the tools used for technical analysis, it's critical to employ key performance metrics like the Sharpe Ratio, Sortino Ratio, and Calmar Ratio to measure risk-adjusted returns. These metrics provide traders with a more comprehensive understanding of how well their strategies balance profits with the risks they are taking. Here's how they apply in real-world trading:

Sharpe Ratio

The Sharpe Ratio is widely used in portfolio management and hedge funds to assess how much extra return is earned for each unit of risk. It's particularly useful when comparing different strategies or funds, as it normalizes returns based on risk. For instance, during the 2008 financial crisis, many portfolios saw negative returns. However, certain hedge funds that maintained a high Sharpe Ratio were able to demonstrate that despite market downturns, their strategies effectively managed risk and delivered returns better than the overall market.

Consider a mutual fund that returns 12% annually. Without context, this return might seem impressive, but if that return was accompanied by high volatility, the risk might not be worth it. Investors and traders use the Sharpe Ratio to assess whether they're being compensated adequately for the level of risk taken. A high Sharpe Ratio indicates that a portfolio is achieving higher returns for less risk, which is crucial for long-term investors like pension funds or endowments that need stable, reliable returns.

In real-world terms, if two investment funds both have similar returns, but one has a significantly higher Sharpe Ratio, professional investors will gravitate toward the one with the higher Sharpe because it means better risk management.

Sortino Ratio

The Sortino Ratio refines the Sharpe Ratio by focusing only on downside risk, ignoring upside volatility, which is generally desirable. This makes it especially relevant for conservative investors who are more concerned with avoiding losses than pursuing aggressive gains. For example, retirees or risk-averse investors often prefer strategies that minimize large drawdowns even if it means sacrificing some upside potential.

In practical application, the Sortino Ratio is frequently used by fund managers to appeal to investors who are sensitive to risk. A hedge fund, for instance, might use the Sortino Ratio to demonstrate that while their returns aren't the highest, their downside risk is very limited, making it an attractive option for risk-conscious clients. This can be particularly important in volatile markets like commodities or emerging markets, where risk mitigation is a priority.

During market corrections, like the tech bubble burst in 2000 or the COVID-19 crash in 2020, funds with a high Sortino Ratio were able to show their investors that they managed to avoid substantial losses even as markets plunged, making them more appealing to risk-sensitive clients. "There's no such thing as a no sale call. A sale is made on every call you make. Either you sell the client some stock or he sells you a reason he can't. Either way a sale is made, the only question is who is gonna close?" - Boiler Room (2000)

Calmar Ratio

The Calmar Ratio is another key metric that compares the average annual return of an investment to its maximum drawdown, making it highly effective in assessing risk during volatile periods. For example, hedge funds that operate in high-risk asset classes like cryptocurrency or speculative tech stocks may use the Calmar Ratio to illustrate how well they've managed extreme market downturns. If two funds have the same return, but one has a much lower maximum drawdown (i.e., it lost less during bad periods), the fund with the higher Calmar Ratio would be seen as the more stable option.

In real-world applications, investors might consider the Calmar Ratio when evaluating long-term performance, particularly in environments where markets experience significant turbulence. For instance, during the 2020 COVID-19 market crash, many funds suffered large drawdowns. However, funds with strong Calmar Ratios were able to highlight their ability to recover from these lows and continue delivering returns, reassuring investors of their resilience.

This is particularly valuable for institutional investors, such as university endowments or insurance companies, which need to maintain a consistent return over time while avoiding significant losses. These institutions often prioritize funds that demonstrate stability and reliability in adverse market conditions, and the Calmar Ratio serves as a key measure in these evaluations.

Real-World Application Summary:

- Hedge funds use the Sharpe Ratio to demonstrate risk efficiency, especially during volatile market phases.
- Risk-averse investors, such as those close to retirement, rely on the Sortino Ratio to ensure downside risk is minimized, making it a favorite for safer investments during uncertain economic times.
- Calmar Ratio is a go-to for assessing resilience during drawdowns, helping long-term investors and funds show how well they manage recoveries after market downturns.

By using these risk-adjusted return metrics, traders and investors can better understand not just the potential for profits, but how well those profits are balanced with risk. This insight allows them to make smarter, more sustainable decisions, especially when navigating volatile or uncertain markets.

Psychological Aspects of Trading

While technical analysis and risk management are vital to successful trading, they are only effective when paired with strong emotional discipline. Trading psychology refers to the emotional and mental state of a trader, which can significantly impact decision-making. The ability to manage emotions like fear and greed, maintain discipline, and adhere to the trading plan is often what separates successful traders from those who fail.

Managing Emotions Like Fear and Greed

Emotional decision-making is one of the primary reasons traders fail. Fear can cause traders to exit positions prematurely, missing out on potential gains, while greed can lead them to hold onto winning trades for too long, risking a market reversal. Both of these emotional extremes can wreak havoc on even the best trading strategies.

Studies by the Behavioral Finance Institute show that traders who experience significant emotional swings—especially during periods of market volatility—are 25% more likely to make irrational decisions, such as abandoning their trading plan or over-leveraging their positions. To counteract this, many traders employ mechanical trading systems or use automated trading platforms to reduce the influence of emotions. A 2021 report from CitiFX noted that traders using algorithmic trading systems reduced emotional decision-making errors by up to 30%, leading to better overall performance.

Developing Discipline and Adherence to the Trading Plan

Discipline is arguably the most important psychological trait a trader can develop. Even the most well-crafted trading strategy will fail if a trader lacks the discipline to follow it consistently. Adherence to the trading plan means not deviating from predefined rules, whether based on indicator signals, risk management techniques, or position sizing.

A disciplined trader will not enter a trade based on a hunch or excitement about market news. Instead, they will wait for clear confirmation from their indicators and ensure that the risk-reward ratio aligns with their plan. According to a 2020 study by the CFA Institute, disciplined traders were 40% more likely to achieve long-term profitability compared to those who frequently altered their strategies based on short-term market movements.

In conclusion, while technical indicators provide critical insights for making informed trading decisions, risk management and trading psychology are just as crucial for long-term success. Effective risk control strategies—such as setting stop-loss levels, proper position sizing, and managing trading capital—help mitigate losses and preserve gains.

Psychological Aspects of Trading

The role of psychology in trading is often underestimated but can be as crucial as technical analysis and risk management. Markets can evoke powerful emotional responses, which can cloud judgment and lead to impulsive decisions. Even with the most robust trading strategy and precise indicators, if a trader cannot manage emotions like fear and greed, the strategy can quickly unravel. Trading psychology encompasses emotional control, discipline, and the ability to stick to a plan, especially when market conditions become volatile. This section delves into the psychological aspects of trading, exploring how emotional awareness and discipline can impact trading success.

Managing Emotions Like Fear and Greed

Emotional responses like fear and greed are natural but can severely impair a trader's decision-making process. Fear can lead to premature exits from trades, while greed may tempt traders to stay in positions longer than their strategy dictates, hoping for more gains. Both emotional extremes can undermine the effectiveness of even the most meticulously crafted trading strategy.

Fear tends to manifest during market downturns or when trades move against expectations. For example, when the market experiences a sharp decline, traders may become overwhelmed by fear and close positions too early, missing potential recoveries. Conversely, greed can drive traders to hold onto profitable trades too long, anticipating additional gains even when indicators signal it's time to exit. Both scenarios highlight the importance of controlling emotional responses to ensure adherence to the trading plan.

In a study published in the Journal of Behavioral Finance, it was found that 60% of retail traders who let emotions guide their trading decisions consistently underperformed compared to those who followed a systematic, indicator-driven approach. The study revealed that traders driven by fear had a tendency to exit trades prematurely 70% of the time, resulting in reduced potential gains. On the other hand, traders motivated by greed often ignored their pre-established exit strategies, leading to higher losses during market reversals. This imbalance underscores the destructive potential of unchecked emotions.

For instance, during the Dot-com Bubble of the late 1990s, many traders held onto stocks far beyond their rational value, driven by greed and fear of missing out (FOMO). As the bubble burst, these traders faced devastating losses. A Harvard Business Review article on behavioral economics from 2002 discussed how traders who could control these impulses by sticking to their technical signals fared better during the market collapse, preserving capital or even profiting by shorting overvalued stocks.

Another example comes from the 2020 COVID-19 market crash, where fear drove many traders to exit positions at the height of the panic, only to miss out on the rapid recovery that followed in the months after. Traders who adhered to their strategies and technical indicators were able to capitalize on market rebounds, as studies show that global equity markets recovered by over 70% by the end of 2020, offering significant upside for disciplined investors.

Developing Discipline and Adherence to the Trading Plan

Discipline is the foundation of successful trading, ensuring that traders adhere to their plan and resist emotional impulses. In volatile markets, it's easy to second-guess strategies, but traders who remain disciplined are more likely to succeed in the long run. Adherence to a trading plan includes respecting pre-established rules, such as sticking to stop-losses, not overriding indicator signals, and avoiding emotional reactions to short-term market fluctuations.

A case study published in Financial Markets and Trading in 2017 illustrated how disciplined traders who adhered strictly to their trading plans and used a blend of indicators (such as moving averages, RSI, and volume indicators) were 30% more likely to maintain profitability compared to those who deviated from their strategies under emotional pressure. The study showed that traders who followed their stop-loss rules and took profits based on indicator signals experienced fewer drawdowns and saw more consistent returns over time.

For example, traders using the RSI (Relative Strength Index) might establish a rule to exit a trade when the RSI reaches 70, indicating overbought conditions. A disciplined trader would follow this signal, even if the trade is currently profitable, to avoid the risk of a sudden reversal. In contrast, an undisciplined trader may choose to hold onto the trade longer, hoping for more profit, only to see the market turn against them, erasing gains.

The importance of discipline can also be seen in algorithmic or systematic trading. In algorithmic trading systems, trades are executed automatically based on predefined conditions, eliminating emotional bias. Research by CitiFX Quantitative Analytics in 2021 showed that algorithmic traders experienced 35% less emotional interference and were more consistent in their application of risk management rules. By sticking to predefined criteria, algorithmic traders outperformed manual traders in volatile markets by a margin of 22%. Don't meet a margin call.

One of the most effective ways to develop discipline is by keeping a trading journal. A trading journal documents every trade, including the rationale behind the decision, the strategy employed, and the emotional state of the trader at the time of execution. A 2020 survey by Trading Psychology Research Institute found that traders who regularly reviewed their trading journals were 25% more likely to avoid repeated mistakes. This practice not only helps to improve discipline but also allows traders to refine their strategies over time.

Another real-world example is the story of Paul Tudor Jones, one of the most successful traders in history. Jones famously adhered to strict stop-loss rules during the Black Monday crash of 1987, which helped him avoid significant losses. His disciplined approach, combined with his use of technical indicators, allowed him to profit massively during one of the worst market crashes in history, reinforcing the value of emotional control and disciplined trading.

In conclusion, managing emotions like fear and greed, while maintaining discipline, is just as important as choosing the right indicators and applying technical analysis. Traders who can master these psychological aspects are more likely to succeed in the volatile and unpredictable world of financial markets.

Integrating indicators into a trading strategy is both an art and a science, requiring a careful balance of technical knowledge, risk management, and psychological control. This chapter has explored how indicators—whether trend-following, momentum, or volume-based—serve as essential tools for navigating different market conditions. However, indicators alone are not enough. Success lies in selecting the right combinations based on market behavior, and then consistently applying them within a structured, well-thought-out trading plan.

Equally critical is the role of risk management, from setting effective stop-loss levels to position sizing, all of which safeguard a trader's capital in unpredictable markets. Furthermore, as emphasized, trading psychology—the ability to control emotions like fear and greed and to adhere to a disciplined approach—can make or break a strategy. While technical indicators offer objective signals, it is the trader's discipline and mental resilience that ultimately ensure long-term success.

By combining the use of indicators with strong risk management and psychological discipline, traders can enhance their ability to navigate the complexities of the financial markets and improve their chances of achieving consistent profitability. Whether you are a seasoned professional or just starting, integrating these elements into your trading strategy will better equip you to face the challenges of the ever-evolving market landscape.

Chapter 9: Case Studies and Practical Applications

In this chapter, we will explore the application of technical indicators in real-world trading scenarios, emphasizing the profound impact these tools can have on both success and failure. While technical analysis is often discussed in theoretical terms, the real challenge lies in its practical application amidst the unpredictable dynamics of financial markets. Through the examination of historical trades, we will uncover how various technical indicators—such as moving averages, Relative Strength Index (RSI), Bollinger Bands, and Fibonacci retracements—can be leveraged to inform decision-making. More importantly, we will also highlight how misinterpretation or improper use of these indicators can lead to poor results, underscoring the importance of discipline and precision in trading.

The focus of this chapter will not only be on the successes achieved through the proper use of indicators but also on the lessons learned from failures. By dissecting both positive and negative outcomes, traders can gain a more comprehensive understanding of how these indicators function in different market conditions, from bullish trends to market crashes and periods of extreme volatility. Whether it's the calculated risks that led to significant gains or the costly mistakes that could have been avoided with better analysis, each case study presented will offer a unique perspective on the power—and limitations—of technical analysis.

Additionally, we will provide **practical tips** aimed at helping traders—particularly those new to the field—avoid common pitfalls. Trading can be a highly emotional and fast-paced environment, where mistakes are often costly, especially for beginners. Missteps such as overtrading, relying too heavily on a single indicator, or failing to implement proper risk management can lead to substantial losses. This chapter aims to equip traders with the tools and knowledge necessary to navigate these challenges with confidence.

Central to this discussion will be the idea of **continuous learning**. The financial markets are dynamic and constantly evolving, influenced by a wide range of factors from technological advances to global macroeconomic events. As such, traders must remain adaptable, always seeking to refine and improve their strategies. This chapter will stress the importance of fostering a mindset that embraces **flexibility** and **innovation** in trading strategies. The ability to pivot in response to changing market conditions, learn from past experiences, and integrate new technologies and indicators into your analysis is critical to long-term success in trading.

In summary, this chapter is designed to bridge the gap between theory and practice, showing how technical indicators can be successfully applied to real-world trading scenarios. Through detailed case studies and practical advice, readers will gain a deeper understanding of how to approach the markets with a balanced, well-informed, and flexible mindset. Whether you are a beginner seeking to build a foundation of trading knowledge or an experienced trader looking to refine your strategy, this chapter will offer valuable insights to enhance your trading journey.

Real-World Examples: Historical Trades and Analysis

Understanding how technical indicators are applied in real-world trading scenarios is crucial for becoming proficient in market analysis. In this section, we will break down significant historical trades, showing the decision-making processes behind them and the outcomes that followed. Each case study will offer valuable insights into how to effectively use indicators and the lessons learned from successes and failures.

Case Study 1: Apple (AAPL) - The 2020 Pandemic Bull Run

Background

At the onset of the COVID-19 pandemic in early 2020, global financial markets faced unprecedented turmoil. The rapid spread of the virus prompted governments worldwide to implement lockdown measures, leading to a significant contraction in economic activity. Apple Inc. (AAPL), recognized as one of the most valuable companies globally, was not immune to this volatility. In February 2020, Apple shares were trading at approximately $320. By mid-March, the stock had plummeted to around $225, reflecting a nearly 30% decline as investors reacted to the uncertainties surrounding the pandemic, including supply chain disruptions and declining consumer demand.

However, as the market adjusted to the new normal, a surprising recovery began to unfold. By mid-2020, several factors contributed to this resurgence:

- **Stimulus Measures:** Governments implemented massive fiscal stimulus packages to support individuals and businesses, boosting investor confidence.

- **Low-Interest Rates:** Central banks around the world slashed interest rates to stimulate borrowing and spending, leading to increased investment in equities.

- **Demand for Technology Services:** With millions of people working from home, the demand for technology products and services surged. Apple, with its robust ecosystem of devices and services, was well-positioned to capitalize on this trend.

By the end of 2020, Apple's stock had soared to record highs, demonstrating the resilience of the tech sector amidst the broader economic challenges posed by the pandemic.

Indicators Used

In navigating this volatile environment, traders utilized several technical indicators to inform their trading decisions:

1. Moving Averages (MA)

- **50-Day Moving Average:** The 50-day MA served as a short-term trend indicator. Traders monitored this average closely to identify potential bullish or bearish shifts in price.

- **200-Day Moving Average:** The 200-day MA acted as a longer-term trend indicator, providing insights into the overall market direction and potential support levels.

2. Relative Strength Index (RSI)

- The RSI is a momentum oscillator that measures the speed and change of price movements on a scale of 0 to 100. It helps traders identify overbought or oversold conditions in the market.

- An RSI below 30 is generally considered oversold, while an RSI above 70 indicates overbought conditions.

3. Fibonacci Retracement Levels

- Fibonacci retracement is a technical analysis tool that identifies potential support and resistance levels based on the Fibonacci sequence.

- Traders commonly use key levels (23.6%, 38.2%, 50%, 61.8%, and 100%) to predict possible reversal points in the price action after significant moves.

Trade Breakdown

The Initial Dip

In March 2020, after witnessing a sharp decline in its stock price, Apple began to stabilize. As the panic selling subsided and markets began to recalibrate, traders who had a solid grasp of technical analysis sought to capitalize on potential buying opportunities.

Identifying the Trend Reversal

- **Crossing Above the 50-Day MA:** By April 2020, AAPL's stock price crossed above the 50-day moving average, signaling a potential trend reversal. This crossover is often regarded as a bullish signal, prompting traders to take positions in anticipation of further price increases.

- **RSI Indicators:** At this point, the RSI hovered around 30, indicating that the stock had been oversold during the preceding market panic. This reading reassured traders that the stock was due for a rebound, reinforcing their decision to enter the market.

Utilizing Fibonacci Levels

- Traders examined Fibonacci retracement levels to identify potential support zones. They noted that the stock found support at the **38.2% retracement level** of its previous uptrend, which aligned perfectly with the observed bullish signals from the MA and RSI.

- This confluence of indicators presented a strong buying opportunity, leading many investors to enter long positions in April.

Rallying to New Heights

As a result of these strategic decisions, investors who purchased AAPL shares in April 2020 and held them until September experienced remarkable gains. Apple's stock price surged, reaching approximately **$360** by early September, reflecting an approximate **60% increase** over just a few months. The combination of strong fundamentals, positive market sentiment, and effective use of technical indicators contributed to this impressive rally.

Key Takeaways

- **Effective Use of Technical Indicators:** The case of Apple illustrates how moving averages and the RSI can serve as powerful tools in identifying trend reversals and assessing market conditions. These indicators allowed traders to make informed decisions amidst a volatile environment.

- **The Importance of Patience:** Traders who remained patient and adhered to their technical strategies were able to avoid the panic selling that characterized the early stages of the pandemic. By waiting for clear signals of a reversal, they capitalized on the recovery.

- **Fibonacci Retracement in Action:** This case also highlights the significance of Fibonacci retracement levels in identifying potential support and resistance areas. Understanding these levels can provide traders with critical insights into market behavior during volatile periods.

- **Strategic Entry Points:** The successful trades in AAPL demonstrate the value of combining multiple indicators for a comprehensive analysis. Utilizing a combination of moving averages, RSI, and Fibonacci levels enabled traders to pinpoint optimal entry points, maximizing potential returns.

- **Continuous Learning and Adaptation:** The volatile nature of financial markets requires traders to remain adaptable and continuously refine their strategies. By learning from past experiences and observing market behavior, traders can enhance their ability to respond effectively to changing conditions.

In summary, the remarkable journey of Apple during the 2020 pandemic serves as a powerful case study in the application of technical analysis. By leveraging key indicators and maintaining a disciplined approach, traders were able to navigate uncertainty and capitalize on a historic market recovery.

Case Study 2: Bitcoin's Historic Rise in 2017

Background

In 2017, Bitcoin (BTC) captured global attention, embarking on an unprecedented bull run that saw its price soar from approximately **$1,000** in January to nearly **$20,000** by December. This meteoric rise was fueled by a confluence of factors, including increased mainstream adoption, heightened media coverage, and rampant speculation among investors.

As Bitcoin began to gain traction, a wave of enthusiasm swept through the cryptocurrency market, attracting both seasoned investors and newcomers alike. Many viewed Bitcoin as a revolutionary technology and a hedge against inflation, particularly in the wake of various geopolitical tensions and economic uncertainties. The allure of quick profits further propelled the frenzy, as individuals and institutions alike sought to capitalize on this emerging asset class.

The Parabolic Rise

- **Mainstream Adoption:** Major corporations and financial institutions began to recognize Bitcoin's potential, with some even announcing plans to accept it as a payment method. The introduction of Bitcoin futures by the Chicago Mercantile Exchange (CME) in December 2017 legitimized the cryptocurrency in the eyes of traditional investors.

- **Media Coverage:** The rapid increase in Bitcoin's price attracted extensive media coverage, creating a feedback loop that generated even more interest and speculation. Social media platforms buzzed with discussions about Bitcoin, further driving the demand.

- **Speculation and Fear of Missing Out (FOMO):** The fear of missing out led many investors to jump into the market without a thorough understanding of the underlying technology or risks, contributing to the parabolic price rise.

However, this explosive growth was not without its pitfalls, as the volatility of the cryptocurrency market began to escalate dramatically.

Indicators Used

To navigate this tumultuous landscape, traders employed several key technical indicators that helped them assess price movements and make informed decisions:

1. Bollinger Bands

- **Purpose:** Bollinger Bands are volatility bands placed above and below a moving average, typically the 20-day simple moving average (SMA). They consist of three lines: the middle line (SMA) and two outer bands that are standard deviations away from the SMA.

- **Application:** During Bitcoin's rise, traders observed frequent touches of the upper band, signaling overbought conditions and increasing market volatility. The widening of the bands indicated heightened market uncertainty and potential reversals.

2. MACD (Moving Average Convergence Divergence)

- **Purpose:** The MACD is a trend-following momentum indicator that shows the relationship between two moving averages of a security's price. It consists of the MACD line, the signal line, and the histogram, which indicates the strength of the momentum.

- **Application:** In 2017, the MACD displayed strong bullish momentum as the MACD line remained well above the signal line, suggesting that the uptrend was intact. However, divergence began to emerge, indicating potential slowing momentum.

3. Volume Indicators

- **Purpose:** Volume indicators measure the number of shares or contracts traded in a security or market during a given period. They are crucial for assessing the strength of price movements.

- **Application:** By analyzing volume, traders were able to gauge the intensity of buying and selling pressure, offering insights into whether a price movement was sustainable or if it was likely to reverse.

Trade Breakdown

The Surge Begins

As Bitcoin's price climbed throughout 2017, traders who monitored the aforementioned technical indicators made crucial observations:

- **Bollinger Bands Signals:** Throughout the year, Bitcoin's price frequently touched the upper band of the Bollinger Bands. These touches indicated that the asset was overbought, prompting traders to assess their positions more critically.

- **MACD Momentum:** The MACD showed a strong bullish trend, with the MACD line remaining significantly above the signal line. This pattern reassured traders that the uptrend was still robust, encouraging them to hold their positions.

Signs of Volatility

As the price approached the **$20,000** mark in December, traders noted crucial shifts in the indicators:

- **Widening Bollinger Bands:** By mid-December, the Bollinger Bands began to widen significantly, indicating increasing volatility in the market. This widening often precedes sharp price movements, serving as a warning signal for potential corrections.

- **RSI Overbought Conditions:** The Relative Strength Index (RSI) surged above **80**, signaling extreme overbought conditions. This level of RSI often suggests that the asset is overvalued, raising concerns about a potential pullback.

- **Volume Indicators:** As December progressed, there was a marked increase in trading volume, particularly during the last week of the month. This surge in volume was accompanied by a shift in the market sentiment, suggesting that selling pressure was mounting.

Profit-Taking Before the Correction

Traders who closely monitored these signals began to take profits before the market correction that followed in January 2018. As Bitcoin reached its peak price, many chose to exit their positions, recognizing the heightened risk associated with overbought conditions and increased volatility.

As anticipated, January 2018 ushered in a significant market correction, with Bitcoin's price plummeting from its nearly **$20,000** high to around **$6,000** by February. Traders who acted on the technical signals were able to protect their profits and avoid substantial losses.

Key Takeaways

- **Effective Use of Bollinger Bands:** The Bollinger Bands provided crucial warnings about increasing volatility and overbought conditions. Traders who monitored these signals were able to adjust their positions proactively.

- **MACD for Momentum Shifts:** The MACD indicator effectively highlighted the early stages of Bitcoin's trend and the subsequent slowdown in momentum. Awareness of these shifts allowed traders to make informed decisions regarding their positions.

- **Volume Indicators Matter:** Increased volume during the last week of December signaled a shift in market sentiment and the potential for a reversal. Understanding volume dynamics is essential for assessing the strength of price movements.

- **Ignoring Signals Can Be Costly:** Traders who overlooked these technical warnings faced significant losses during the January 2018 crash. This case study underscores the necessity of heeding technical indicators, particularly during euphoric market phases.

- **Continuous Learning and Adaptation:** The rapid changes in the cryptocurrency market necessitate continuous learning and adaptation. Traders must remain vigilant and responsive to evolving market conditions to protect their investments and capitalize on opportunities.

In summary, Bitcoin's historic rise in 2017 serves as a compelling case study in the effective application of technical analysis. By leveraging indicators like Bollinger Bands, MACD, and volume analysis, traders could navigate the frenzy surrounding cryptocurrencies and make informed decisions that preserved their capital and maximized their returns. This case underscores the importance of remaining disciplined, informed, and adaptive in a highly volatile market.

Case Study 3: Tesla (TSLA) - A Study in Breakout and Volatility (2020)

Background

In 2020, Tesla Inc. (TSLA) emerged as one of the most spectacular success stories in the stock market, with its share price skyrocketing by over **700%** from January to December. The surge in Tesla's stock price was driven by several key factors that created a perfect storm for growth:

- **S&P 500 Inclusion:** In December 2020, Tesla was officially included in the S&P 500 index, a significant milestone that legitimized the company's position in the market and attracted considerable institutional investment.

- **Strong Delivery Numbers:** Tesla consistently reported impressive delivery numbers throughout the year, exceeding market expectations. In the third quarter alone, the company delivered over **139,000** vehicles, marking a record for quarterly deliveries and bolstering investor confidence.

- **Optimism About Electric Vehicles:** As the world increasingly shifted toward renewable energy and electric vehicles (EVs), investor sentiment surrounding Tesla grew more bullish. The global push for sustainability and stricter emission regulations fueled optimism about the future of electric vehicles, particularly Tesla's market-leading position.

- **Retail Investor Interest:** The rise of retail investors, spurred on by trading platforms like Robinhood, further amplified the buying frenzy. The meme stock phenomenon surrounding Tesla, fueled by social media platforms, contributed to its dramatic price increases.

As a result of these factors, Tesla's stock price, which started the year around **$430**, approached **$2,000** by late August 2020. This chapter will delve into the technical indicators that traders used during this tumultuous period to navigate the volatility and make informed decisions.

Indicators Used

To capitalize on Tesla's extraordinary growth, traders utilized several key technical indicators:

1. Volume-Weighted Average Price (VWAP)

- **Purpose:** VWAP is a trading benchmark that measures the average price a security has traded at throughout the day, based on both volume and price. It provides a clearer picture of the stock's trend strength, especially in intraday trading.

- **Application:** In Tesla's case, the stock consistently traded above the VWAP, indicating strong buying interest and a bullish trend. Traders often use VWAP to identify potential support and resistance levels.

2. Parabolic SAR (Stop and Reverse)

- **Purpose:** The Parabolic SAR is a trend-following indicator that helps traders identify potential reversal points in the price of an asset. The indicator appears as dots above or below the price chart, depending on the trend's direction.

- **Application:** In the context of Tesla, the Parabolic SAR remained below the price during the bullish trend, suggesting that the trend was intact. A flip of the indicator above the price often signifies a potential reversal, serving as a critical exit signal for traders. Be willing to admit when you're wrong and exit a trade.

3. Relative Strength Index (RSI) and Moving Averages

- **Purpose:** The RSI is a momentum oscillator that measures the speed and change of price movements, providing insights into overbought or oversold conditions. Moving averages help smooth out price data to identify the overall trend direction.

- **Application:** During Tesla's rise, the RSI fluctuated in the **70-80** range, indicating overbought conditions but also confirming the strength of the upward trend. Moving averages helped traders confirm the bullish momentum and provided additional signals for entry and exit points.

Trade Breakdown

Breakout Above $1,000

In early July 2020, Tesla's stock price broke through the significant psychological barrier of **$1,000**. Traders employing technical analysis closely monitored the following signals:

- **VWAP Confirmation:** As the stock surged past this key level, it consistently traded above the VWAP, indicating strong buying interest and momentum. This scenario reassured traders that the bullish trend was likely to continue.

- **RSI Levels:** During this period, the RSI hovered in the **70-80** range, suggesting that while the stock was becoming overbought, the upward momentum remained robust. Traders interpreted this as a signal to stay long, confident in the continued demand for Tesla shares.

- **Parabolic SAR Alignment:** The Parabolic SAR remained below the price, further confirming the bullish trend. This alignment gave traders confidence that the uptrend was strong and that they could hold their positions without fear of an imminent reversal.

Approaching $2,000 in August

As Tesla's price approached the **$2,000** mark in August, traders began to observe critical shifts in the indicators:

- **RSI Reaches Overbought Territory:** The RSI began to indicate extreme overbought conditions, crossing above **80**. Traders familiar with RSI interpretations recognized this as a warning sign that the stock might be due for a correction.

- **Widening Volatility:** As the price surged, volatility increased, and the potential for a sharp pullback became more apparent. Traders used this knowledge to reassess their positions and prepare for possible corrections.

- **Parabolic SAR Flip:** By mid-August, the Parabolic SAR flipped above the price, serving as a signal of a potential trend reversal. This shift prompted many traders to consider taking profits, as the bullish trend may have been losing steam.

Avoiding the September Correction

Traders who had been monitoring these technical indicators closely made strategic decisions based on the emerging signals:

- **Profit-Taking Strategies:** Recognizing the potential for a correction, many traders exited their positions, locking in gains before the anticipated downturn. This foresight proved invaluable as Tesla's stock subsequently dropped over **30%** in September, falling from approximately **$2,000** to around **$1,400**.

- **Managing Risk:** The combination of VWAP, RSI, and Parabolic SAR allowed traders to manage their risk effectively in a highly volatile environment. By recognizing signs of trend exhaustion, they could navigate the market fluctuations with greater confidence.

Key Takeaways

- **VWAP as a Trend Indicator:** The consistent trading of Tesla above the VWAP provided traders with a clear indication of bullish momentum, enabling informed decision-making.

- **Parabolic SAR for Trend Reversal:** The Parabolic SAR effectively identified potential trend reversals, allowing traders to time their exits strategically and avoid significant losses during corrections.

- **RSI for Overbought Conditions:** The RSI served as a valuable tool for identifying overbought conditions during Tesla's rapid ascent. Traders who acted on these warnings could secure profits before market corrections occurred.

- **Recognizing Trend Exhaustion:** The ability to recognize signs of trend exhaustion, combined with a thorough understanding of technical tools, is critical for managing risk in volatile, high-growth stocks like Tesla.

- **Continuous Monitoring:** The fast-paced nature of the stock market demands continuous monitoring of technical indicators. Traders who remain vigilant and responsive to market signals can better navigate periods of extreme volatility.

In summary, Tesla's extraordinary rise in 2020 exemplifies the effective application of technical analysis in a high-volatility environment. By utilizing indicators such as VWAP, Parabolic SAR, and RSI, traders could navigate the excitement surrounding Tesla's stock and make informed decisions that preserved capital and maximized returns. This case underscores the importance of combining various technical tools to manage risk and capitalize on market opportunities in the rapidly changing landscape of high-growth stocks.

Practical Tips and Common Mistakes

In the fast-paced and often unpredictable world of trading, beginners can face numerous challenges that can lead to costly mistakes. To help navigate these pitfalls, this section provides practical tips aimed at fostering disciplined trading practices and enhancing overall performance. By following these guidelines, novice traders can build a strong foundation for their trading journey and increase their chances of success.

Tips for Beginners to Avoid Common Pitfalls in Trading

1. Start Small and Gradually Increase Position Sizes

Overview: One of the most significant mistakes beginners make is jumping into the market with large positions. This approach amplifies risk exposure and can lead to substantial losses. Trading is inherently risky, and inexperienced traders are more susceptible to making impulsive decisions under pressure.

Actionable Advice:

- **Begin with a Small Investment:** Start with a minimal portion of your trading capital, allowing you to learn the ropes without jeopardizing your financial health. A common rule is to limit your initial position to **1-2%** of your total capital.

- **Incremental Increases:** As you gain experience and confidence in your strategies, gradually increase your position sizes. Use a structured approach, such as the **Kelly Criterion**, to help determine the optimal size of your bets based on your trading performance.

- **Reflect on Experience:** After each trade, regardless of its outcome, take time to reflect on what you learned. Did your analysis hold true? Did you follow your plan? This self-reflection will build your confidence and inform your decision-making in future trades.

2. Don't Overtrade – Be Selective with Your Trades

Overview: Overtrading is a common pitfall for beginners, often stemming from the desire to always be in the market or from emotional reactions to price movements. This behavior can lead to higher transaction costs, increased stress, and a diluted focus on quality trades.

Actionable Advice:

- **Set Trade Criteria:** Develop a clear set of criteria for entering trades. This may include specific technical signals, market conditions, or fundamental data. Stick to these criteria to avoid making impulsive decisions.

- **Quality over Quantity:** Focus on high-probability trades that align with your analysis and indicators. Aiming for just a few well-researched trades each week can be more beneficial than multiple trades based on hunches or market noise.

- **Use a Trading Plan:** A well-defined trading plan serves as a roadmap for your trading activities. Include your trading goals, strategies, and risk management rules. This plan will help keep you disciplined and focused on executing your trading strategy effectively.

3. Master a Few Indicators First

Overview: With an overwhelming number of technical indicators available, beginners often make the mistake of trying to use too many at once. This can lead to analysis paralysis and confusion, making it difficult to make informed decisions.

Actionable Advice:

- **Focus on Key Indicators:** Start by mastering a few essential indicators that are widely used and easy to understand. Recommended indicators include:

- **Moving Averages (MA):** Help identify trends and potential reversal points.

- **Relative Strength Index (RSI):** Measures momentum and indicates overbought or oversold conditions.

- **Volume Indicators:** Assess the strength of price movements and confirm trends.

- **Understand the Context:** For each indicator you choose, take the time to understand how it works and what it indicates. Research how to interpret signals from these indicators in the context of the overall market environment.

- **Gradually Expand Your Toolkit:** Once you feel comfortable with a few indicators, you can begin to explore additional tools and techniques. Always prioritize understanding how each indicator contributes to your overall analysis.

4. Use Stop-Loss Orders

Overview: Effective risk management is crucial in trading. One of the simplest yet most powerful tools for managing risk is the use of stop-loss orders. A stop-loss order automatically closes your position when a stock reaches a certain price, helping to limit potential losses.

Actionable Advice:

- **Determine Your Risk Tolerance:** Before placing a trade, decide how much you are willing to risk on that particular position. A general guideline is to limit your risk to **1-2%** of your total trading capital on any single trade.

- **Set Appropriate Stop-Loss Levels:** Place your stop-loss order at a logical level based on technical analysis—often just below a key support level or a predetermined percentage below your entry price. Adjust your stop-loss as the trade becomes profitable to protect your gains.

- **Avoid Moving Your Stop-Loss:** One common mistake is moving stop-loss orders further away from the current price in the hope that the market will turn around. This behavior can lead to larger losses. Stick to your original plan.

5. Avoid Emotional Decision-Making

Overview: Emotions can significantly cloud judgment, leading to impulsive buying and selling decisions. Fear and greed are two primary emotions that often derail a trader's strategy, causing them to deviate from their trading plan. *"The point is, ladies and gentlemen, that greed, for lack of a better word, is good. Greed is right, greed works. Greed clarifies, cuts through, and captures the essence of the evolutionary spirit. Greed, in all of its forms; greed for life, for money, for love, knowledge has marked the upward surge of mankind." - Wall Street (1987)*

Actionable Advice:

- **Stick to Your Trading Plan:** Having a well-defined trading plan helps you maintain focus, even during volatile market conditions. Review your plan regularly to ensure it aligns with your trading goals.

- **Practice Mindfulness:** Engage in mindfulness techniques, such as meditation or deep-breathing exercises, to help manage stress and maintain emotional control during trading sessions.

- **Limit Exposure to Market Noise:** Avoid excessive news consumption or social media discussions that may provoke emotional responses. Set specific times to check news or market updates to reduce the risk of emotional trading.

6. Keep a Trading Journal

Overview: Keeping a trading journal is a vital practice for continuous improvement. Documenting your trades and the thought processes behind them helps identify patterns in your decision-making and performance.

Actionable Advice:

- **Record Every Trade:** Include essential details such as entry and exit points, position sizes, the rationale for each trade, and the indicators used. Be honest about your emotions and decisions during the trade.

- **Analyze Your Performance:** Regularly review your trading journal to identify patterns in your successes and failures. Look for recurring mistakes or misjudgments and consider how you can improve your strategies moving forward.

- **Set Goals for Improvement:** Use insights from your journal to set specific, measurable goals for your trading practice. For example, aim to reduce emotional trades or increase the win rate of your selected trading strategy.

By adhering to these practical tips and recognizing common pitfalls, beginner traders can cultivate disciplined habits and improve their overall trading performance. Trading is a continuous learning process, and by focusing on developing skills, strategies, and emotional resilience, traders can navigate the complexities of the market with greater confidence.

Emphasis on Continuous Learning and Adapting Strategies

1. The Market is Constantly Evolving

Financial markets are dynamic, with new trends and technologies emerging regularly. To stay competitive, traders must continuously learn and adapt their strategies. This could involve staying updated with economic news, studying new technical indicators, or learning how to trade new asset classes such as cryptocurrencies.

2. Adaptation to Changing Market Conditions

Markets are not static, and strategies that worked in a trending market might fail in a sideways or volatile market. For example, **moving averages** are effective in trending markets but may give false signals in a choppy, range-bound environment. Traders should constantly reassess the effectiveness of their strategies and make adjustments based on the current market conditions.

3. Leverage New Technologies

Technological advancements such as algorithmic trading, machine learning, and artificial intelligence are reshaping how trades are executed. Traders who can leverage these technologies to their advantage will have a competitive edge in the market. Invest in companies with a solid competitive advantage.

4. Join Trading Communities

Engaging with a community of traders allows you to exchange ideas, learn from others' experiences, and stay informed about new strategies and tools. Many successful traders collaborate with peers to fine-tune their approach and keep each other accountable for their trades.

5. Stay Humble and Keep Learning

Even the most successful traders experience losses. The key to long-term success is learning from mistakes and remaining humble. The market is a challenging environment, and overconfidence can lead to significant losses. Approach each trade with caution and respect for the inherent risks involved.

This chapter has illustrated the importance of real-world application of technical indicators and the insights gained from historical trades. From Apple's pandemic recovery to Bitcoin's 2017 bull run and Tesla's volatility in 2020, each case study demonstrates the power of combining different indicators to make informed trading decisions.

By understanding common mistakes and adopting practical tips, beginner traders can mitigate risks and improve their chances of success. Continuous learning, adapting to new market conditions, and embracing new technologies are essential for staying competitive in the evolving world of trading.

Conclusion

As we conclude this exploration of trading strategies, indicators, and case studies, it is essential to reflect on the future directions in trading. The trading landscape is continuously evolving, shaped by emerging trends and technologies that promise to transform how traders analyze markets and execute trades. The rise of artificial intelligence and machine learning is revolutionizing trading analysis, allowing for more sophisticated algorithms that can process vast amounts of data in real time. These technologies enable traders to identify patterns and trends that may not be visible through traditional analysis methods, thereby providing a significant edge in decision-making. Additionally, advancements in data visualization tools are enhancing traders' ability to interpret complex market information quickly and efficiently. As platforms become increasingly user-friendly and accessible, more individuals are entering the trading arena, leading to a democratization of trading that fosters diverse perspectives and strategies. Moreover, the integration of social trading networks allows traders to share insights and strategies, further enriching the collective knowledge within the trading community.

In light of these advancements, it is crucial for aspiring traders to develop their own unique trading styles and strategies tailored to their personal goals, risk tolerance, and market understanding. This process of self-discovery is integral to becoming a successful trader. It involves not only learning from the successes and failures of others but also critically analyzing one's own experiences. Building a robust trading strategy takes time and experimentation; thus, beginners should be patient with themselves as they refine their approaches. Engaging with various indicators and methodologies can provide invaluable insights into what works best for each trader's individual circumstances.

As we look ahead, the journey of trading is not merely about financial gains; it is about cultivating a mindset of discipline, curiosity, and continuous learning. New traders should remind themselves that setbacks and challenges are part of the process. Each trade presents an opportunity to learn and improve, whether it results in a profit or a loss. Remaining committed to honing one's skills and understanding the markets is essential for long-term success. The world of trading is filled with complexities and nuances, but it is also rich with opportunities for those willing to invest the time and effort to learn. By embracing a mindset of lifelong learning and adaptability, traders can navigate the ever-changing market landscape with resilience and confidence. "Life's tough.....it's even tougher if you're stupid." - John Wayne

In summary, while the path to becoming a successful trader may be fraught with challenges, it is also one of immense potential for growth and achievement. By leveraging emerging technologies, developing personalized strategies, and maintaining an unwavering commitment to learning, traders can position themselves to thrive in the dynamic world of financial markets. Remember that every expert was once a beginner; thus, your journey is just as valuable as your destination. Embrace the process, stay disciplined, and keep your curiosity alive—these qualities will serve as your guiding principles as you embark on your trading journey.

Book Blurb

Robust trading programs are instrumental in navigating the complex and often volatile financial markets.

They offer a structured and disciplined approach to trading, leveraging advanced algorithms and data analysis to identify potential opportunities and manage risks. Their value to traders and investors is multi-faceted and can significantly impact their financial outcomes.

1. Enhanced Decision-Making: Robust trading programs utilize sophisticated algorithms that analyze vast real-time market data. This allows for identifying patterns, trends, and anomalies that may not be readily discernible through manual analysis. By leveraging these insights, traders can make more informed and data-driven decisions, reducing the influence of emotions and impulsive actions.

2. Risk Management: One of the primary benefits of robust trading programs is their emphasis on risk management. These programs often incorporate stop-loss orders, position-sizing strategies, and other risk mitigation measures to protect capital and minimize losses. By adhering to predefined risk parameters, traders can avoid catastrophic drawdowns and preserve their investments.

3. Increased Efficiency: Manual trading can be time-consuming and prone to errors. Robust trading programs automate many aspects of the trading process, from order execution to portfolio rebalancing. This saves time and ensures that trades are executed swiftly and accurately, taking advantage of fleeting market opportunities.

4. Diversification: A well-designed trading program often incorporates diversification strategies, spreading risk across various asset classes and markets. This helps to reduce overall portfolio volatility and mitigate the impact of adverse events in any single market.

5. Backtesting and Optimization: Robust trading programs are typically backtested on historical data to assess their performance under various market conditions.

This allows for the identification of strengths and weaknesses and the optimization of parameters to improve future results.

6. Adaptability: Financial markets are constantly evolving. Robust trading programs are often designed to adapt to changing market dynamics, adjusting their strategies based on new information and trends. This adaptability helps to maintain consistency in performance over time.

7. Emotional Discipline: Emotions can be a trader's worst enemy. Fear and greed can lead to irrational decisions that jeopardize profits. Robust trading programs operate based on predefined rules and parameters, eliminating emotional biases and ensuring discipline in trading activities.

8. Transparency and Accountability: Reputable trading programs provide transparency into their methodologies and performance. This allows investors to understand the underlying strategies and track the program's progress, fostering trust and accountability.

9. Accessibility: Trading programs are no longer limited to institutional investors. Many platforms and software providers offer robust trading tools to individual traders, democratizing access to sophisticated trading strategies.

In conclusion, robust trading programs offer a valuable tool for traders and investors seeking to navigate the complexities of financial markets. By enhancing decision-making, managing risk, increasing efficiency, and promoting discipline, these programs can significantly improve trading outcomes and contribute to long-term economic success. As technology continues to advance, the role of robust trading programs in shaping the future of finance is only expected to grow.

We aren't always 100% correct, but we are entirely computerized and math-based. We follow a systematic, unemotional approach to trading with clearly defined risk parameters.

We would be lying if we told you we were always 100% correct.

We aren't, but we are:

Entirely computerized and math-based...

100% systematic and unemotional...

Even though they are 100% defined risk-specific

Markets traded:

CBOT 10-year Note

CME Japanese Yen

CME Euro Currency

CBOT Soybeans

CBOT Soybean Meal

CBOT Soybean Oil

CBOT Corn

CBOT Wheat

Cliff Notes

Technical Indicators: Mining the Secrets of Price Action

Technical indicators are more than mathematical formulas; they are powerful tools that allow traders to delve into the psychology of the market and decipher the language of price action. Derived from historical data, these indicators provide a lens through which traders can identify patterns, gauge momentum, and anticipate future price movements.

Why are Technical Indicators Essential?

- Decoding Market Sentiment: Indicators act as a sentiment barometer, revealing the collective psychology of traders and investors. By understanding how others react to price movements, traders can gain an edge in anticipating future market direction.

- Objective Analysis: While fundamental analysis relies on subjective interpretation of financial data, technical indicators offer a more objective approach. They provide quantifiable price action measurements, reducing emotional biases and promoting disciplined decision-making.

- Pattern Recognition: Indicators help identify recurring patterns in price charts, such as head and shoulders, double tops, and flags. Recognizing these patterns can provide valuable clues about potential trend reversals or continuations.

- Early Warning System: Certain indicators act as an early warning system, signaling potential trend changes before they become apparent to the naked eye. This allows traders to adjust their positions and capitalize on emerging opportunities proactively.

- Risk Mitigation: Indicators can help traders define entry and exit points, set stop-loss orders, and manage risk effectively. By incorporating indicators into their trading strategy, traders can minimize potential losses and protect their capital.

Delving Deeper into Indicator Categories:

1. Trend-Following Indicators:

These indicators help traders ride the waves of market trends, capturing profits as prices move sustainably.

- **Moving Averages (MA):**

o Beyond the Basics: Explore different moving averages, such as Exponential Moving Average (EMA) and Weighted Moving Average (WMA), to understand how they assign weights to recent price data. Experiment with various periods to identify the optimal settings for different trading styles and market conditions.

o Dynamic Support and Resistance: Moving averages can act as dynamic support and resistance levels. In an uptrend, prices tend to bounce off rising MAs, while in a downtrend, they often face resistance at declining MAs.

o Crossover Strategies: Develop trading strategies based on MA crossovers. For example, a bullish crossover occurs when a short-term MA crosses above a long-term MA, signaling a potential uptrend.

- **MACD (Moving Average Convergence Divergence):**

o Histogram Interpretation: Pay close attention to the MACD histogram, which plots the difference between the MACD and signal lines. The histogram provides insights into a trend's strength and momentum.

o Divergence Analysis: Master identifying divergences between the MACD and price action. A bullish divergence occurs when the MACD forms higher lows while the price forms lower lows, suggesting a potential bullish reversal.

o Fine-tuning Parameters: Experiment with different settings for the fast and slow-moving averages used to calculate the MACD. This can help optimize the indicator for different timeframes and trading styles.

- **Average Directional Index (ADX):**

o Trend Strength and Volatility: Combine ADX with other indicators, such as the Plus Directional Indicator (+DI) and Minus Directional Indicator (-DI), to determine a trend's strength and direction.

o Identifying Ranging Markets: Use ADX to identify ranging or sideways markets. Low ADX values often indicate a lack of clear trend, suggesting that range-bound trading strategies may be more suitable.

2. Momentum Indicators:

These indicators provide insights into the speed and magnitude of price changes, helping traders identify potential overbought or oversold conditions.

- **Relative Strength Index (RSI):**

o Failure Swings: Learn to recognize failure swings, which occur when the RSI fails to reach a previous high or low, signaling a potential trend reversal.

o Hidden Divergences: Explore the concept of hidden divergences, which can provide early warning signs of trend continuations. A bullish hidden divergence occurs when the RSI forms lower lows while the price forms higher lows.

o Customization: Adjust the RSI period to fine-tune its sensitivity. Shorter periods (e.g., 7 or 14) are more sensitive to recent price changes, while more extended periods (e.g., 28) provide a smoother indicator.

- **Stochastic Oscillator:**

o Overbought/Oversold Zones: While the traditional overbought level is 80 and the oversold level is 20, consider adjusting these levels based on the specific security and market conditions.

o %K and %D Crossover: Develop trading strategies based on crossovers between the Stochastic Oscillator's %K and %D lines. A bullish crossover occurs when the %K line crosses above the %D line.

- **Commodity Channel Index (CCI):**

o Trend Confirmation: Use CCI to confirm trend direction and strength. In an uptrend, the CCI tends to stay above zero, while in a downtrend, it tends to remain below zero.

o Identifying Extreme Movements: CCI can help identify extreme price movements that may be unsustainable. High CCI readings suggest the price is significantly above its average, while low readings indicate the opposite.

3. Volatility Indicators:

These indicators measure the degree of price fluctuations, helping traders assess risk and identify potential breakouts or reversals.

- **Bollinger Bands®:**

o Volatility Breakouts: Develop trading strategies based on volatility breakouts. A breakout above the upper Bollinger Band can signal a continuation of an uptrend, while a breakout below the lower band can signal a continuation of a downtrend.

o Band Width: Pay close attention to the width of the Bollinger Bands. Expanding bands suggest increasing volatility, which can create trading opportunities, while contracting bands suggest decreasing volatility, which may lead to range-bound price action.

o M-Tops and W-Bottoms: Learn to recognize M-tops and W-bottoms, chart patterns that can form within Bollinger Bands, and signal potential trend reversals.

- **Average True Range (ATR):**

o Position Sizing: Use ATR to determine appropriate position sizes based on the security's volatility. Higher ATR values warrant more minor positions to manage risk effectively.

o Trailing Stop-Loss: Incorporate ATR into your trailing stop-loss strategy. For example, in an uptrend, you could set a trailing stop-loss at a multiple of the ATR below the current price.

4. Volume Indicators:

These indicators analyze trading volume to assess the strength of price movements and identify buying or selling pressure.

- **On-Balance Volume (OBV):**

o Confirmation of Price Trends: Use OBV to confirm the validity of price trends. A rising price trend accompanied by a rising OBV suggests intense buying pressure and a healthy trend.

o Divergence Analysis: Look for divergences between OBV and price action. A bullish divergence occurs when the OBV forms higher lows while the price forms lower lows, suggesting potential buying pressure and a possible trend reversal.

- **Accumulation/Distribution Line (A/D Line):**

o Identifying Accumulation and Distribution: Use the A/D Line to identify periods of accumulation (buying pressure) and distribution (selling pressure). A rising A/D Line suggests that institutions and informed traders are accumulating the security.

o Confirmation of Breakouts: The A/D Line can help confirm the validity of breakouts. A breakout above a resistance level accompanied by a rising A/D Line increases the likelihood of a successful breakout.

- **Money Flow Index (MFI):**

o Identifying Money Flow: Use MFI to assess money flow into and out of a security. High MFI values suggest intense buying pressure, while low values suggest strong selling pressure.

o Overbought/Oversold Conditions: Similar to the RSI, the MFI can be used to identify potential overbought and oversold conditions. However, in strong trending markets, the MFI can remain overbought or oversold territory for extended periods.

Elevating Your Technical Analysis:

- Combining Indicators: Don't rely on a single indicator. Use multiple indicators from different categories to confirm signals and gain a more comprehensive market view.

- Contextual Awareness: Always consider the broader market context and underlying fundamentals when interpreting indicator signals. Technical indicators should be used in conjunction with other forms of analysis to make informed trading decisions.

- Adaptive Approach: Recognize that market conditions are constantly changing. Be prepared to adjust your indicator settings and trading strategies as needed.

- Continuous Learning: The world of technical analysis is vast and ever-evolving. Stay curious, explore new indicators, and refine your understanding of existing ones.

Traders can gain a significant market edge by mastering technical analysis and effectively utilizing indicators. Remember that technical indicators are not a crystal ball but a robust set of tools to help you navigate the complexities of price action and make more informed trading decisions.

For more information, contact

Home - Intermarket Outlook

-30- My name is, John Connor

"I'll be back!!"

intermarketoutlookllc@gmail.com

630 822 6949 (Cell)

www.ingramcontent.com/pod-product-compliance
Lightning Source LLC
LaVergne TN
LVHW060038210926
848481LV00013B/3902
9798227225047